Deseret Book Company
Salt Lake City, Utah

Special appreciation is expressed to the contributers to this work for their willingness to share their thoughts and testimonies with youth. Each author accepts complete personal responsibility for the material contained within his or her chapter. There is no endorsement for this work (real or implied) by The Church of Jesus Christ of Latter-day Saints, the Church Educational System, or Brigham Young University.

Chapter 2, "Recognizing and Following the Spirit," by Diane Bills, is adapted from the talk tape "Making Life Count," by Diane Bills, produced and published by Covenant Communications, Inc., and is used by permission.

Library of Congress Catalog Card Number: 96-84075

ISBN 1-57345-160-6

Printed in the United States of America

10   9   8   7   6   5   4   3   2   1

CONTENTS

1

PLAYING WITH FIRE

Art E. Berg

The pilot's somber voice came over the intercom, "Ladies and gentlemen, this is your captain speaking. We are experiencing some difficulty with the landing gear . . . "

After traveling more than 200,000 miles a year as a professional speaker, I was not prepared to hear words like that. I had boarded Delta's flight 1691 out of the Salt Lake City International Airport. My destination was Idaho Falls, Idaho, where I was to meet with one of my clients. The flight was to be relatively short with just one brief stop, in Jackson, Wyoming.

I had been enjoying some polite conversation with a businessman seated next to me as the plane began its gradual descent into the Jackson Hole area. Somewhere in the midst of going through his lineage, I felt the plane begin to rise again. I glanced toward the window.

The pilot, speaking over the intercom, explained that they were experiencing some trouble with the landing gear. Continuing, he said, "We will fly on to Idaho Falls to give us more time to work on the problem." We felt relieved. A short time later, the plane began its descent toward the Idaho Falls airport. Within minutes, I felt us ascending again. Now I knew we were in trouble.

The captain spoke: "We are having trouble getting the landing gear in the nose to go down. We have tried it electrically and manually. However, we have no indication as to whether the wheel on the front is in position and locked. We are returning to the Salt Lake City airport. This will allow us to consume most of our fuel. Salt Lake has a longer runway and is much better equipped to handle an emergency landing such as this."

The mood was heavy. Passengers stole glances at one another as if to question whether all of this was really happening. The captain continued, "Please listen carefully to the flight attendants, who will give you instructions on how to prepare for an emergency landing." They had my undivided attention.

The flight attendants explained the routine. Eyeglasses were to be removed and placed in your sock. Neckties should also be taken off. Pockets should be emptied of pens, pencils, and other sharp objects. Seat belts must be tightened. We were told that the captain would command, "Brace yourself! Brace yourself! Brace yourself!" prior to impact. We were then to immediately put our heads down and clasp our hands behind our knees.

The captain explained that in his attempt to land, he would hold the front wheel off of the runway for as long as he could. However, when the front wheel made contact with the pavement, we should probably expect it to collapse under the weight of the aircraft. The plane would slide on its belly along the runway until it came to a stop. He told us that the emergency doors would be opened, chutes would inflate, and we were to evacuate immediately.

As we approached the Salt Lake City International Airport, the flight attendant stopped at my seat and inquired, "Do you have any questions or concerns, Mr. Berg?" Calmly I replied, "Yes, I really have just one concern: now, am I getting all of my frequent flier miles for this trip? I mean, after all, we flew all the way up to Idaho Falls and back again!" The look on her face implied that perhaps I was asking the wrong kind of question.

Hearing my attempt at humor, the gentleman seated next to me politely asked, "Aren't you at all worried?" I responded, "No, not really. I figure that when my number is up, my number is up. The only thing that really worries me is that *your* number might be up. I think you should save the rest of us by doing the courageous thing and *jumping!*" He laughed, and the tension seemed to be temporarily relieved.

The pilot's voice broke our moment of peace: "We will fly by the control tower at an extremely low altitude so that they can do a visual of our landing gear and can confirm whether or not it is even down. However, even if it is down, we have no indication that it is locked in position." As we streaked by the tower, we looked out our windows at the runway below. The runway had been closed off to all other air traffic. From one end to the other, it was lined with ambulances, fire trucks, and emergency vehicles. Traffic on the nearby interstate highway had stopped on the shoulder of the road to observe such an unusual landing.

Sitting near the front of the aircraft, I had the advantage of looking back down the aisle of the Boeing 737 and glancing into the eyes of the hundred or more passengers. Some were teary-eyed; others stared blankly forward. Some used conversation with those around them to relieve the tension, while many more contemplated their future in silence. Some were eagerly using the in-flight phone system to call loved ones, while others quietly sobbed. Was I really prepared to die? Sober thoughts.

My thoughts were interrupted with the harsh command, "Brace yourself! Brace yourself! Brace yourself!" My head lunged forward. I clasped my hands firmly behind my knees. I felt the rear wheels of the plane make contact with the runway and heard the shrill screech of rubber on asphalt. The nose stayed aloft for an unusually long period of time. However, as our speed fell to less than 125 miles per hour, the front wheel hit the runway. I held my breath. The landing gear was locked!

As the plane came to a stop, the passengers erupted into spontaneous applause. Some embraced, while others whispered silent prayers of thanks and gratitude. Flight 1691 was over but would not soon be forgotten.

Life is tenuous and fragile. There are no guarantees. Some live long and healthy lives, while others are seemingly cut short. I did learn one very valuable lesson: although we may not be able to pick the hour of our departure from this world, we can choose how well prepared we are. I silently vowed to make better choices.

On July 2, 1994, a fire broke out near Glenwood Springs, Colorado, from a lightning strike in an area that had been plagued by drought and unusually high temperatures. At first, the fire was paid very little attention. Other fires within the region seemed more important because more homes and livestock were at risk. However, within twenty-four hours, the little, unimportant fire had spread out of control.

On July 3, 1994, smoke jumpers and helicopter tactical teams were dispatched to make preparations for containing the fire. Three days later, July 6, 1994, a severe weather front moved into the area with winds of 40 to 60 miles per hour. The fire was advancing at 1200 feet per minute (nearly a four-minute mile). Firefighters were forced to run across steep, rough terrain. The flames were being fed by scrub oak, which in that area was extremely dry and volatile and was burning at temperatures of up to 1700 degrees. What began as a twenty-acre blaze quickly spread to 1800 acres in three hours. Tragically, fourteen firefighters lost their lives when the fire suddenly turned on them and they were unable to outrun it.

What happened? What went wrong? These were not inexperienced firefighters. All but one of the firefighters who died had more than six years of experience; one had fifteen years. In independent studies surrounding the tragedy, researchers identified several reasons why the fire-fighters lost their lives. Perhaps there is a lesson to be learned about the value of being prepared.

1. Firefighters did not maintain adequate lines of com-munication. A firefighter's first duty in battling a forest blaze is to establish a single radio channel as a direct line for communication with the base, supporting aircraft, and other firefighters. Unfortunately, in their eagerness to fight Mother Nature, these firefighters failed to select a clear channel as the main line for communication. Because four different agencies were involved in the battle, firefighters were communicating on four different channels.

A "red flag warning" had been issued for the area fore-telling a quickly approaching, dangerous weather front with high winds. With firefighters operating on four dif-ferent channels, only a small number ever received ade-quate warning to clear the area.

We get ourselves into spiritual trouble when we do not have an open, direct line of communication with our Heavenly Father. We find ourselves at risk when we listen to competing communication from our peers, the media, and Satan himself. During times of peace or storm, we need to keep the channel clear, awaiting inspiration, instruction, and encouragement from our Father above. We keep the channel open when we seek Him in daily prayer and quiet meditation.

2. The firefighters did not have a watchman established. Firefighters help keep themselves safe when they establish a watchman. This individual sits at the optimal vantage point to observe wind direction, approaching weather fronts, hot spots, and the speed of the burn. A watchman communicates directly with the firefighters, warning them

of impending danger, suggesting strategy, and recommending escape routes. The watchman has the advantage of viewing things from a distance, which makes it possible for him to get the *big* picture.

In the tragedy of the Glenwood Springs fire, no watchman was established. As a result, several of the firefighters ran directly into the fire because they could not determine the direction it was traveling the fastest. No "red flag warnings" were communicated. No updated weather reports were given. No continuing status was reported on the terrain and type of fuel burning. The firefighters were left to fight alone.

Fortunately, the Lord has established a system of watchmen for you and me. They are called prophets and Church leaders. They have the unique advantage of seeing that which we are unaware of. They warn us of impending danger and counsel us on codes of conduct and behavior. We put our spiritual lives at risk when we ignore the watchmen.

3. The doomed firefighters were found to have broken ten fundamental rules of firefighting and to have ignored eighteen warning signs. Among the mistakes they made were these:

In the firefighters' haste to do battle, they never established any escape route or safe zones. A firefighter always needs a place to go to when the fire turns on him. A firefighter needs to be prepared for any change in weather or wind direction. Before fighting the blaze, the firefighter knows to set up specific escape routes, safe zones, and contingency plans. The firefighters who lost their lives at Glenwood Springs had failed to do so.

Second, many of the firefighters broke one of the cardinal rules when they attempted to escape the fire by running uphill. Fire burns faster uphill. Firefighters are taught to run across a hill or down it, but not up. Two men died only 100 feet from the top of a hill. If they had run across the hill, they might have survived.

Third, a firefighter, when the fire turns on him, knows to immediately abandon his backpack. A backpack loaded with all the equipment a firefighter would need can weigh as much as 120 pounds. Unfortunately, most of the men evidently underestimated the danger they were in; most of those who died were found with their backpacks still on.

Fourth, they did not take the time to understand the nature of the wood that was burning. The scrub oak had only a third as much moisture as a normal tree. Because of the dryness of the wood, it burned hotter and faster than expected. Firefighters carry fire shelters with them. If a fire turns on them, they can quickly put the shelter over them and let the fire burn past. The shelters can withstand heat of up to 1000 degrees. Because of the extremely dry nature of the scrub oak, the heat was as high as 1700 degrees. Several firefighters died in their shelters.

Many years ago, an unusual book was written entitled *A Chance World*. In this fictitious world, every day was new and different. Life was spontaneous and creative. The opportunity to acquire new knowledge every day was guaranteed. In the morning you never knew if the sun would come up or whether the moon and stars would appear. When it rained, you weren't sure if water would fall from the skies, or literally cats and dogs. When you planted an apple seed in the ground, you would have to wait to see if you got apples or oranges or pears or nothing at all. Seasons of the year came and went by chance. Nobody knew when to plant or when to harvest. And so everybody did nothing at all.

Although each day carried the excitement of being spontaneous and new, people couldn't count on anything. New knowledge had little value because it never stayed the same—there was no truth. Fortunately, you and I do not live in a fictitious world of chance. We live in a world that is created, organized, and governed by laws: laws we can count on and live by.

We protect ourselves through obedience to the laws that the Lord has given us. My brother, Paul, taught me a valuable lesson one day when we were driving through a neighborhood together. I was driving about ten miles per hour over the speed limit when a child darted out into the street from between two parked vehicles. I swerved quickly and fortunately I missed hitting the child—but only by inches. My heart was racing.

In frustration I yelled, "Stupid kid! Watch where you're going!" My brother glanced over at me and simply said, "You know, Art, if you had hit the kid, it would have been your fault." I was astounded! How could it have been my fault? He responded, "If you hadn't been speeding, you would have had more time to react. By speeding, you stepped outside the protection of the law. You would have been responsible."

I had never thought of it that way. The laws are here to protect us, not punish us. When we choose to disobey, we step outside the protection and blessings of the law and put ourselves at risk. Obedience to the Lord's laws is critical to being prepared.

I have a friend who hates his job. He dislikes everything about it. Every time I talk to him he tells me more and more about what is wrong with his employer. He can't stand his office; it's too small. He dislikes and distrusts his co-workers. He loathes his boss. After listening to his complaints for several months I finally asked him, "If you hate your job so much, why don't you just quit? This is America. Go somewhere else. Do something else." Do you know what he said? "'Cause I only got fifteen years left!"

Flight 1691 was a reminder; we don't know how much time we have left. Use your time wisely. Keep the lines of communication open with your Heavenly Father through daily prayer. Establish a watchman by heeding the counsel of the prophets and your Church leaders. And keep yourself safe from the fires of sin through strict obedience to the laws with which God has blessed us.

Art E. Berg is a professional motivational speaker and president of Invictus Communications, Inc. He is the author of *Some Miracles Take Time* and *Finding Peace in Troubled Waters: 10 Life Preservers for When Your Ship Springs a Leak*. He enjoys wheelchair rugby, parasailing, boating, and traveling. Art and his wife, Dallas, have two children.

2

RECOGNIZING AND FOLLOWING THE SPIRIT

Diane Bills

It was the toughest class I had taken yet in high school—chemistry! My dad, a nuclear engineer, required all of his children to take it before graduating.

Kim and I hurried home from school. We had a huge chemistry assignment due the next day, which would count heavily toward our final grade. When we got home we went into my room, giggling and laughing, hoping to postpone doing this awful assignment. Finally we opened our books to begin. The material just didn't make sense to me. Kim was having the same difficulty. We tried for what seemed hours to figure out the problems. As dinnertime approached we hadn't made any headway. We needed to hurry because that evening we had Young Women's at seven o'clock.

As the time approached for us to go to Young Women's, we still hadn't completed any of the chemistry. We decided to stay home and get it done. We'd have to miss Young Women's this week.

As that decision was made, I remember feeling awful inside. Kim and I looked at each other. She was having the same uneasy feeling.

"We'd better go to Young Women's," I said. Kim agreed.

The peace that came with that decision was overwhelming.

It was close to nine o'clock when we got home. We knelt down and offered a prayer that went something like this: "Heavenly Father, we went to Young Women's tonight; we did what we felt was the right thing to do. Please help us now with this assignment . . ."

As Kim and I opened our chemistry books to begin working, a miracle took place. The problems that had seemed so foreign hours before suddenly made sense.

"Kim, I understand this!" I yelled.

"So do I!" she said.

We began writing as quickly as we could, completing the assignment in about twenty minutes. We were not surprised the next day when we got perfect scores on our papers. We knew in our hearts that it was because we had followed the Spirit and done the right thing.

"I, the Lord, am bound when ye do what I say; but when ye do not what I say, ye have no promise" (D&C 82:10).

In the parable of the ten virgins, the Savior spoke of his second coming and those who would be ready when he comes.

"Then shall the kingdom of heaven be likened unto ten virgins, which took their lamps, and went forth to meet the bridegroom.

"And five of them were wise, and five were foolish.

"They that were foolish took their lamps, and took no oil with them:

"But the wise took oil in their vessels with their lamps.

"While the bridegroom tarried, they all slumbered and slept.

"And at midnight there was a cry made, Behold, the bridegroom cometh; go ye out to meet him.

"Then all those virgins arose, and trimmed their lamps.

"And the foolish said unto the wise, Give us of your oil; for our lamps are gone out.

"But the wise answered, saying, Not so; lest there be not enough for us and you: but go ye rather to them that sell, and buy for yourselves.

"And while they went to buy, the bridegroom came; and they that were ready went in with him to the marriage: and the door was shut.

"Afterward came also the other virgins, saying, Lord, Lord, open to us.

"But he answered and said, Verily I say unto you, I know you not.

"Watch therefore, for ye know neither the day nor the hour wherein the Son of man cometh" (Matthew 25:1–13).

In speaking of virgins, the Lord was referring *only* to members of the Church. He clearly indicated that when he comes, many members of the Church will be unprepared to meet him.

Not all of us will have enough oil to make our lamps burn bright enough to light the way when he comes. After learning that concept, I desired greatly to know what the light represents, and what the oil is that keeps the light burning bright.

Jesus gave us the answer many hundreds of years later. He gave it to the Prophet Joseph Smith in 1831, when He said, "And at that day, when I shall come in my glory, shall the parable be fulfilled which I spake concerning the ten virgins. For they that are wise and have received the truth, *and have taken the Holy Spirit for their guide,* and have not been deceived—verily I say unto you, they shall not be hewn down and cast into the fire, but shall abide the day" (D&C 45:56–57; emphasis added).

The key words in this scripture are these: "and have taken the Holy Spirit for their guide." The light on the lamp, which guides our way, is the Holy Spirit or the Holy Ghost. The oil that keeps the light burning bright is everything we do in our lives that is righteous, which allows the Spirit to burn bright within us. Each time we pray, read the scriptures, fast, think loving thoughts, or humble ourselves before the Lord, we add oil to our lamps. When we live a commandment, go to the temple, or show love, concern, and understanding to others, we add to our store of oil. On the other hand, when we give in to worldly enticements, such as going to an R-rated movie or to a questionable party, or going to a bar, casino, or other unholy place where the Spirit cannot dwell, we are turning our lamps over and letting the oil spill out. When we say or do unkind things to our parents or siblings, the oil starts draining. When we listen to profane music, indulge in vulgar behavior, or take harmful things into our bodies, we are emptying oil from our lamps. The Holy Ghost will be a light to guide our path only if we live righteously.

The Spirit speaks to us most often through our feelings, or impressions spoken softly to our minds. The scriptures are replete with examples:

"And when ye shall receive these things, I would exhort you that ye would ask God, the Eternal Father, in the name of Christ, if these things are not true; and if ye shall ask with a sincere heart, with real intent, having faith in Christ, he will manifest the truth of it unto you, by the power of the Holy Ghost. And by the power of the Holy Ghost ye may know the truth of all things" (Moroni 10:4–5).

"Did I not speak peace to your mind concerning the matter? What greater witness can you have than from God?" (D&C 6:23).

Here is the key. If a decision makes you feel good, peaceful, or content, then move ahead; if it leaves you feeling uneasy, doubtful, or unsettled, then beware.

John had finally turned sixteen years old. He couldn't wait to find employment, so that he could have some spending money of his own. He decided to go to the nearby Arby's restaurant to apply for a job. John presented himself well in the interview, and before he knew it the manager had offered him the position. John was excited! The manager gave him some instructions concerning the job and explained what commitments would be required. One of those commitments was to work many Sundays. As John listened, something inside didn't feel right. He felt uneasy and uncomfortable. He really wanted the job, yet he knew deep down inside that working on Sundays was wrong. The uneasy feeling persisted.

John finally turned to the manager and explained that he would have to turn the job down. He really wanted it, but it was important to him to go to his church on the Sabbath and to honor that day by not working. John left the restaurant. He was disappointed to miss out on the job, but inside a light was shining bright. He knew that he had made the right decision. He felt peaceful and calm. The Holy Ghost had shown him the way, and, most important, John had followed those feelings.

The next day John received a call from the manager at Arby's. "You know," he said, "I am really impressed with you. I admire a young man who would stand up for his values. I'm going to give you the job anyway, *and* I will make sure you never have to work on Sundays."

John was thrilled to get the job, but he would have felt that inner peace even if he had not been called back. The light of that right choice was more important to him than any job.

"I, the Lord, am bound when ye do what I say; but when ye do not what I say, ye have no promise."

Angie and her date arrived at the theater with the two other couples in their group. They found good seats inside and made themselves comfortable. Angie was having a great time until the movie began. Everything was all right for a while, but suddenly some scenes came up on the screen that made her feel extremely uncomfortable, scenes she knew she should not be polluting her life with. She turned to her date and whispered that the movie was making her uncomfortable and that she would wait in the lobby for him and the others. Then she had the additional courage to quietly get up and walk out by herself.

In the lobby, Angie was at peace inside. As embarrassing as it had been for her to get up and leave, she knew she had done the right thing.

Within a very short period of time, her date joined her in the lobby. He told her how proud he was of her for having the courage to get up and leave. They would wait together for the others. It wasn't long until couple number two joined them, and shortly couple number three came out of the theater as well. Because one young woman chose to follow the light of the Spirit inside of her, she became an example to others.

"I, the Lord, am bound when ye do what I say; but when ye do not what I say, ye have no promise."

Shortly after my college years, I attended a wedding reception with a young man I was dating at the time. The groom was a convert to the LDS faith, and none of his family were members of the Church.

We arrived toward the close of the reception, and we were famished. We hadn't eaten for hours.

"I sure hope they have good refreshments," I said. My date definitely agreed.

The line had just broken up, but we were lucky to catch the bride and groom. We chatted with the family members and then hurried off for those refreshments.

As we sat down in the serving area, we noticed there was hardly anyone around. We waited and waited and waited. After a while one of the servers came out around the corner and said, "Oh, sorry, they've put all the food away."

How disappointing for two starving young adults. But then we spotted an ice-cream slush in a large punch bowl on the other side of the room. We jumped to our feet and made a beeline for it. Yes! There was still something for us to eat! My date served me first and then himself. Just as I was lifting the glass to my mouth something inside said, "Stop!" I stopped, looked at the glass, then at my date, and noticed he was putting his cup down as well.

"I don't think we're supposed to drink this," I said.

He looked at me and said, "I think you're right."

Just then the groom's father ran across the room to warn us. "Don't drink that," he said. "It's loaded with alcohol."

It is humbling to know that the Holy Ghost will not only guide us but protect us and keep us clean, if we will listen.

"I, the Lord, am bound when ye do what I say; but when ye do not what I say, ye have no promise."

Jared was a senior at one of the prominent high schools in Utah. He was very athletic and had been chosen to play on the varsity basketball team. That year, at a basketball camp his team attended at BYU, Jared had a humbling experience. At the beginning of the week the staff of the camp announced that they were looking for a team or a young man that exemplified strong values, good sportsmanship, and all-around outstanding character. They would watch all participants throughout the week and give a large cash award to the person or the team that was selected.

Partway through the week, Jared and his teammates spent a free evening playing a card game in their dorm. In this game a person would shout a vulgar word each time he got a match. As the game began, Jared felt uneasy. Something inside was telling him that this was offensive to God. He knew it was wrong. It came his turn. Instead of calling out the vulgarity that the others had used, Jared said a funny word. His teammates looked at him strangely. Then, surprising to him, many of his teammates began using the funny word that Jared had used. He had truly set a righteous example for the others. Jared was glad he had

had the courage to follow the Spirit. Inside he felt at peace for his choice.

The end of the week arrived, and the big announcement from the staff came. What team would get the cash award? They all hoped it would be theirs. Speaking into the microphone, the director of the camp said that the staff had decided not to give the award to a team this year, but felt they had found a person who reflected the outstanding character they had sought for. Jared's name was announced.

Those coaches and staff members were not present on the night that Jared and his friends were playing the game of cards. They didn't know about that specific example of Jared's courage. What they had noticed was his overall character. One thing I truly believe is that when a young person is moral in the small areas of life, it shows up in all the larger areas. Jared simply stood out. There was something about Jared that felt right. That something right was the Holy Ghost shining brightly within him.

"I, the Lord, am bound when ye do what I say; but when ye do not what I say, ye have no promise."

Diane Bills, a full-time homemaker and part-time motivational lecturer, enjoys writing, crafts, and calligraphy. She served a mission to Belgium and graduated from the University of Utah. She and her husband, Christian, have three children. Her essay is taken from the talk tape "Making Life Count," by Diane Bills, produced and published by Covenant Communications, Inc.

3

WHILE LIFE HANGS IN THE BALANCE

David L. Buckner

As I held him in my arms, I could hear that his breathing was labored and heavy. His little hands curled around my finger and his small chest heaved in and out, crackling like a fire with every breath. Every few minutes he would awaken with a gasping cough and a choking scream. Each movement he made startled me and reminded me that he was there in my arms. I had not slept for three days but had held my little boy close to my heart, frightened that he would not take the next breath. Frightened that his little five-month-old body could not handle the violent cough, the fluid that was building in his lungs, or his rising temperature. Hour after hour I watched him as day melted into night and back again to daylight. While the clock made another revolution, I continued to sit in the same chair, rocking my child and hoping for a quick recovery.

I thought back to the day he arrived in this world, his tiny little cry and wide-eyed stare. He was as perfect a child as any parent could wish for. Everything about him was beautiful, perfect, and completely innocent. As the cool air in the delivery room entered his lungs for the first time, he let out a scream that announced his arrival and introduced him into a mortal world, a world unlike anything he had ever experienced. For many years he had been held back to come to earth at this time. He had awaited his turn and now he had finally entered this world where he would be given the opportunity to make choices, to learn right from wrong, and to make mid-course corrections when he strayed. Unlike his previous experience, he would be a witness to violence and pain, anger and hate, persecution and prejudice, and his body would experience disease and the discomforts of mortality. His memory of his previous experience was now erased as his earthly test began.

All of these memories of his birth faded away as he awoke again in my arms, wheezing and gasping for air. Lifting him upward, I gently patted his back and silently prayed for him to be well. I knew his body was adjusting to earth life by forming necessary antibodies against disease, but I still wanted him well, healthy, and happy. He settled once again in my arms and closed his eyes. I could still hear him wheeze and feel the sweat on the back of his neck as the fever worsened. The room was dark, with only the city lights shining through the window. Joshua's eyes were shut now, and for the first time in three days he was resting calmly in my arms. As I sat motionless, staring out the window, my racing heart calmed and the many tears I had shed worrying about my son dried on my cheeks. In the silence of the night I felt alone, unable to understand how life could twist and turn from one day to the next. *With all the spiritual disease in the world today, how can I ever raise this little boy to be a warrior of the last days,* I wondered.

My silent reflection did not go unanswered. There was a quiet peace that filled the room, a peace that only the Spirit could provide. It seemed like it had been so long since I had felt the Spirit that strongly. And now, in a time of need I knew it was present and could feel its warmth and calming influence. As it entered the room I recalled the wonderful promise given to us by the Lord, "Pray always, and I will pour out my Spirit upon you, and great shall be your blessing—yea, even more than if you should obtain treasures of earth" (D&C 19:38).

Pray always, and I will pour out my Spirit upon you, I thought. What a simple yet powerful promise. For three days I had paced the front-room floor worrying about my son, called doctors and nurses for advice, and considered every alternative mankind could offer. But in my haste to find an immediate remedy, I had thought little of the Lord's promise, "Pray *always,* and I will pour out my Spirit upon you." Sitting there in the dark of the night, holding my sick child in my arms, I needed the promised comfort from the Spirit. I closed my eyes, took several deep breaths, and began to send my heartfelt prayers heavenward. Quietly I sat pouring my heart out to my Father in Heaven. "How can I help this little child to live a long and healthy life?" I asked. "How can I protect him from sickness and disease and from all the dangers of the world and keep him safe from everything out there that would take away his happiness? How can I teach him about our heavenly home, our heavenly parents, and the sacrifice of our Elder Brother Jesus Christ? And what if he strays—how can I help him find his way back to the only pathway leading to true happiness and eternal life?"

With so many questions on my mind, I left my prayer unfinished, listening intently for an answer. I held Joshua closer and stared silently at the lights that lit up the evening sky outside our New York City apartment. The tall buildings outside our window looked like beacons on a hill, pointing their lights toward heaven. While Joshua lay quietly in my arms, a light in a far-off window flickered, dimmed, and finally went out. It wasn't alone. Other lights from other buildings began to turn off one by one, and finally the shiny white lights on the sky-scraping Chrysler Building dimmed and sputtered out as the city went to sleep. I had never been awake to witness the end of a day in a big city like New York. I began to reflect on the significance of such an event. As bright and beautiful as the lights of the city seemed, they were still temporary fixtures, capable of being extinguished one by one. Created to resemble the light of the daytime sun, their existence is temporary, man-made, and designed to only imitate nature's beauty and God's eternal gift of light. The life span of these artificial lights is short and their power is limited. Unlike God's eternal light, they can only promise darkness at the end of their short lives.

Although I had not continued a verbal conversation with my Father in Heaven, the two-way communication of my prayer was now taking place. As my son lay sleeping in my arms, my mind had reflected on the many important questions in life. In the silence of the night the Spirit was now tutoring and teaching me. "He that asketh in Spirit shall receive in Spirit" (D&C 46:28). The simple message of the Spirit that night was clear. My questions now began to be answered and the Spirit began to confirm the power of the message, a message I now share with you.

1. *"Life is temporary; search for that which is eternal!"* Although our earthly experiences are often exciting, frequently challenging, and many times thrilling, they are only temporary moments in time, a flickering light in a distant building. Yet we often focus on those fleeting flashes of light and lose our eternal perspective, blinded for the moment by the man-made glimmer of brilliance. And in the end, the light goes out, and we are left with only the charred remains of our temporary experience. But this does not have to be. Our course in life is ours to chart, and the paths we take are ours to choose. It is our personal video we are creating in life, and only we can determine what will be played back at the end of our earthly experience. Indeed, all that we do on earth is recorded in heaven,

for better or worse, and we are the creators of the story that is told.

The newspaper headline was short and concise: "Burger Bandits Caught on Tape." This was not the first time video surveillance cameras had caught someone in the act of a crime. But it was the first time the bandits had taken such foolish pride in their work, forgetting the consequences of such actions. Four young kids had made a habit of breaking into restaurants late at night, fixing themselves dinner, and leaving before daybreak. But one night they discovered they were on video and began an elaborate role play for the camera. Completely oblivious to the consequences of their actions, they stood before the camera interviewing one another as if reporting for the local news channel. One by one they gave their names, addresses, and telephone numbers and discussed at some length their previous crimes. Just as the last interview was completed, the lock on the front door of the restaurant turned and the youths escaped out the back door. It wasn't long before the police had viewed the video, arrested the kids, and charged them with a number of crimes in the area. The final comment made by the local police chief was one to be remembered by all. He said, "Police work has never been easier. All we had to do was tell them to wave at the camera."

No matter where we are or what we are doing, our life is being recorded. We are making choices every day that will show up on our eternal video. All too often we are making those choices alone, without consulting our Father in Heaven or requesting a confirmation of the Spirit. As a worthy young latter-day warrior, you are entitled to the promptings of the Spirit. The Lord reminds his worthy servants that "as often as thou hast inquired thou hast received instruction of my Spirit" (D&C 6:14). Every day you must begin your search for that which is eternal by calling on the Spirit to guide you through the day. "Put your trust in that Spirit which leadeth to do good—yea, to do justly, to walk humbly, to judge righteously; and this is my Spirit" (D&C 11:12).

2. *"You write your story—search for the Spirit to teach you."* As a young boy I would often go to the neighborhood park to play baseball. I was never very good and hated it when I was up to bat. I would always get nervous and stand there waiting for George, the neighborhood big brother, to throw the three strikes, so I could sit back down. Every time I got up to bat, the outfield players would yell, "Get in closer, he won't hit it too far." The whole outfield would come in ten yards just in case I connected with the ball. This would make me extra nervous, and I would swing more furiously and miss the ball by an even greater margin. This daily after-school ritual made living in the neighborhood very difficult during baseball season. The more I would try, the more my friends would give me advice. "Stand tall! Eye on the ball!" they would yell. "You can do it, Buck, just keep your head up." With all their comments, I often felt like a pretzel by the time I unwound my swing after missing the ball. One day after school, George and his little brother Clark took me aside and tried to teach me how to swing at the ball. "Watch the ball, watch the ball, watch the ball," they repeated. No matter how hard I tried, I couldn't keep my eye on the ball when it got close to the wood of the bat.

One day I decided I had had enough of neighborhood baseball. I went down to the baseball diamond and made my declaration loud and clear. "I hate baseball, and I think you are all really terrible friends! I never want to play again, and I don't care if I ever see you again!" With that I picked up my bat, turned around, and ran all the way home. I was frustrated and angry but had made up my mind to never play again.

For several days I went straight home from school. As I approached the park on my way, I could hear my friends cheering and chanting but kept my resolve never to go back to the park. Arriving at home, I set out to play my own game of baseball. I took my bat into the backyard and started hitting pop flies. After a few swings and fewer hits, I set the bat down and walked around the yard picking up the baseballs. I made it halfway around the yard and then sat down underneath our big maple tree. *This just isn't working,* I thought. I could see there was no way I could learn to play baseball without a team. And although my friends weren't always perfect teachers or coaches, they nevertheless constituted a team. Recognizing how important it was to belong to a team, I jumped to my feet, grabbed my bat and mitt, and ran across the street to resume my place at first base. That day I learned there is no substitute for membership on a team.

We all need to understand the importance of building and maintaining our eternal team. Father in Heaven knew how hard it would be to participate in life alone, so he provided us with a team in the form of a family. Every team takes on a different appearance, but we are all part of a chosen team, and we have all been given a charge to build and strengthen our team. We are asked to overlook the imperfections of our teammates and work to develop a perfect team. "The ultimate purpose of every teaching, every activity in the Church is that parents and their children are happy at home, sealed in an eternal marriage, and linked to their generations" (Boyd K. Packer, *Ensign,* May 1994, p. 19).

Elder Packer also warned that the adversary will do anything and everything to break up the team and force us to play alone. "The ultimate purpose of the adversary, who has 'great wrath, because he knoweth that he hath but a short time,' is to disrupt, disturb, and to destroy the home and the family." Every day we see evidence that the family team is under attack. Consider some of the evidence:

• 40 percent of homes in America do not have a father living in the home

- 70 percent of juvenile delinquents come from father-less homes
- 80 percent of all births in the inner cities of America are out of wedlock
- 50 percent of all marriages in America end in divorce
- A child is neglected or abused every 47 seconds in America

My young friend, build your family team. Strengthen your home by participating in family home evening. Overlook the imperfections of your team members and focus on building one another rather than allowing the adversary to win. Prepare for and insist upon a holy temple marriage. Never settle for the temporary and terminal earthly approach to marriage, which assures a divorce at death. And never quit the team. Your search for the eternal reward can never be fully realized if you quit.

3. *"Build and maintain your eternal team."* I boarded the plane and took my seat. I had taken the flight many times and was not looking forward to the five hours it would take to reach my destination. I sat back and began to flip through a magazine provided by the airline. The gentleman sitting next to me appeared to be weathered and full of life's experiences. His black shirt was pulled up on his arms far enough to reveal several large, rather grotesque tattoos. From his ears dangled two round rings, and every finger on both hands was adorned with gold and silver rings. He smelled of smoke, and, hiding behind big dark glasses and a cowboy hat, he seemed quite satisfied to remain silent during the flight. I continued to leaf through the magazine until he leaned over and broke the silence by introducing himself. I responded, and we began to talk about the weather, flying, and our reasons for making the trip.

The conversation continued until take-off, when we both fell silent and returned to our own thoughts and reflections. After a short nap I awoke for the dinner service, and we again began to talk. He asked why I didn't accept the wine that had been offered. I told him I was a member of The Church of Jesus Christ of Latter-day Saints and that as a young man I had made a decision not to drink. He was amazed and began to inquire about my other beliefs. Our lengthy discussion turned to living a moral life and my determination to stay faithful to my wife and family. I described the other standards of the Church and told him of my desire to return to my heavenly family after this life.

The discussion slowed down, and my new friend became more silent and apparently less interested. I finished expressing my last thought and returned to my magazine. Almost an hour passed before he spoke again. I feared that maybe I had said too much. Sometimes in our enthusiasm to share the gospel we forget that people need to be spoon-fed rather than force-fed. As I continued to thumb through the pages, my new friend turned to me and asked, "So how do you know when you are doing what's right? How does anyone know what is right?" The question took me by surprise. Because I had always relied upon my conscience to discern right from wrong, I didn't know how to respond.

It was the first time I had actually met someone who had lost his sense of conscience. He could no longer discern between right and wrong. His earthly experience had numbed him to the extent that he was past feeling. This man was like Laman and Lemuel of old, who were told, "And he hath spoken unto you in a still small voice, but ye were past feeling, that ye could not feel his words" (1 Nephi 17:45). Indeed, from what he had told me about himself, he appeared to have been enticed with the promise of fame, riches, and power. He had been deceived by the adversary who would call "evil good, and good evil" (Isaiah 5:20).

My young friend, do not allow yourself to become numb to the Spirit. There is a spiritual disease that the adversary uses to infect the conscience. It is a disease that removes the light of Christ from us and suggests that there is no right or wrong, black or white, only shades of gray. This is not the case. We must always remember that they are still the Ten Commandments, not the "ten suggestions." It is still the law of chastity, not a recommendation on morality. And it is still the Word of Wisdom, not a commentary on good health.

4. *"Keep the light within lit and avoid spiritual disease."* Three hours had passed and Joshua had not moved in my arms. His temperature had dropped and his breathing was less labored and heavy. I bowed my head and thanked my Father for his love, his concern, and his answers to my heartfelt prayer. He had answered each of my questions. He had calmed my fears and concerns and had taught me the importance of listening to the Spirit. As the morning light began to shine through the window, I again reflected upon the day my little boy came to the earth and on his tiny cry and wide-eyed stare. But now I saw him as much more than my little boy. He came with a great purpose. "The great purpose of the work in which we are engaged is to help each of us along the way of immortality and eternal life" (Gordon B. Hinckley, *Ensign*, November 1995, p. 89). Our lives hang in the balance. We must diligently search for that which is eternal. My prayer is that we will make it together. To that end, may I set forth a challenge:

1. Search for that which is eternal.

2. Pray always for the Spirit to teach and guide you.

3. Build and maintain your eternal team.

4. Keep the light within constantly burning.

I sincerely pray that we may all return to our heavenly family and participate in that great reunion with our Father in Heaven and our Elder Brother Jesus Christ.

David L. Buckner holds bachelor's, master's, and law degrees from Brigham Young University and teaches part-time on the faculty there. An avid skier, he has been a ski instructor for seven years. He loves to travel, scuba dive, play tennis, and speak to the youth of the Church. David is married to the former Jennifer Jackson.

4

UNDERSTANDING THE ATONEMENT

Stace Hucks Christianson

It has been some years now since I sat in my living room with the parents of some teenagers and had a discussion about chastity. We talked about the challenges that the royal generation faces and the growing strength of the opposition. Since I hadn't had the experience of raising my own teenagers yet, I sat quietly and mostly listened to the experiences of those loving parents as they voiced their concerns and searched for solutions. They talked about the need for education and clearer boundaries, more firesides, lessons, and youth conferences focused on teaching the law of chastity to the youth of the Church. As I sat there listening I reflected on the comments that my seminary students often made. "We get so sick of everything being focused on the law of chastity. We've gotten the message; we know when we are living it and we know when we're not." It was then that I asked myself: Why do the adults feel as though the youth aren't getting enough direction and guidelines, while the youth are complaining that they are getting too much?

I went home that night seeking answers to that question. Answers rarely come to me suddenly. I have found that I must be very patient and persistent in my search for truth.

So I was not surprised that it took several months to make an important discovery: I was reading in Alma 39, the part where Alma confronts his son Corianton about the son's immoral behavior. It is interesting that Corianton received more counsel from his father than any of the prophet's other sons. What struck me, though, was that in the four chapters of counsel only a few beginning verses addressed the broken law itself. The bulk of what Alma had to say was about the Savior and the effect of His atoning sacrifice. As I reflected upon what I had read, I thought about my experiences with my students in seminary, and I realized that what enables us to live righteously is not our devotion to the commandments, but our devotion to Christ. If we love and desire to serve him, keeping his commandments is a joy and not a task.

This reminded me of what Nephi taught. "We know that it is by grace that we are saved, after all we can do. And, notwithstanding we believe in Christ, we keep the law of Moses, and look forward with steadfastness unto Christ, until the law shall be fulfilled. For, for this end was the law given; . . . And we talk of Christ, we rejoice in Christ, we preach of Christ, we prophesy of Christ, and we write according to our prophecies, that our children may know to what source they may look for a remission of their sins. Wherefore, we speak concerning the law that our children may know the deadness of the law; and they, by knowing the deadness of the law, may look forward unto that life which is in Christ, and know for what end the law was given. And after the law is fulfilled in Christ, that they need not harden their hearts against him when the law ought to be done away" (2 Nephi 25:23–27).

This is the kind of devotion that is anchored in an intimate relationship with the Savior, and that kind of devotion makes it easy to put his will and desires first. Those of my students who were succeeding in living righteously were able to do so because at some point they had drawn close to him and experienced a personal outpouring of his love. It followed that they, like Nephi, wanted to return a portion of that love to him. A desire to surrender our rebellious wills to Christ is a characteristic of his disciples. And one of the consequences of such a surrender is a change of heart, something King Benjamin's people experienced after their conversions. "The Spirit of the Lord Omnipotent, which has wrought a mighty change in us, or in our hearts, that we have no more disposition to do evil, but to do good continually" (Mosiah 5:2). (Notice that the change of heart is brought about by "the Spirit of the Lord.")

Again, it was months later that I was reading in the Pearl of Great Price, in the book of Moses, when I noticed that Moses asks the Lord God a very significant question. He says, "Tell me concerning this earth, and the inhabitants thereof, and also the heavens" (Moses 1:36). In other words, what is the Lord's purpose for the inhabitants of the earth? And God answers, "This is my work and my glory—to bring to pass the immortality [to live forever] and eternal life [to live like God and live with him forever] of man" (Moses 1:39). To bring eternal life to us required that several things be accomplished. First, that God create a place where he could send us to experience mortality. Second, the creation of a plan that would provide a way for us to be redeemed from death and sin and become like him. Such a plan would need to provide or preserve knowledge, free agency, opposition (in order to have one of those three we must have the other two; they are inseparable), joy, the ability to procreate, a body, and, eventually, a perfect and resurrected body capable of withstanding God's presence. This plan is called the plan of salvation or the plan of redemption (see Alma 12:33).

One of the reasons I feel such passion toward the things that follow in this chapter is because I love discovering the unchanging truths of the gospel. In our church we have very strong traditions and a rich culture. There are Church policies that can help us and give us guidelines, but they are all subject to change. The doctrines and principles discussed in this chapter are eternal truths, which means they are not subject to change. They must be understood if we are to be saved. You will find them consistent in the eternities. They are the most fundamental aspects of our belief system in the gospel of Christ, and, when studied, the most fascinating and profound.

The Old Testament introduces the three pillars of salvation. The first pillar is the Creation, the second pillar is the Fall, and the third pillar is the Atonement. Consider this series of questions, which I will later answer.

1. "What is the purpose of the Creation?"

2. "What does the Creation have to do with the plan of salvation?"

3. "How does the Creation affect me daily?"

4. "What does the Fall have to do with the plan of salvation?"

5. "How does the Fall affect me daily?"

6. "What does the Atonement have to do with the plan of salvation?"

7. "How does the Atonement affect me daily?"

If you want, you can search for the answers yourself. Look in the following scriptural chapters: 2 Nephi 2 and 9 and Alma 12 and 40–42.

What is the purpose of the Creation? Heavenly Father created the earth so that we might have a place to live and to work out our salvation by learning to choose good instead of evil. But what about the purpose of *our* creation? When Christ appeared to the Nephites he asked them, "What manner of men ought ye to be? Verily I say unto you, even as I am" (3 Nephi 27:27). The purpose of our creation is to eventually become like Heavenly Father and his son Jesus Christ, in other words, perfect (see Matthew 5:48; 3 Nephi 12:48). As mentioned earlier, knowledge, free agency, and opposition are all vital components in the process of eternal progression.

What does the Creation have to do with the plan of salvation? When Satan tempted Eve in the Garden of Eden, he told her that if she would partake of the tree of knowledge of good and evil, she would be as the Gods, knowing good and evil, and that she would not die as a consequence. Like many of Satan's lies, it was only half a lie. It was true that if Eve partook of the fruit she would gain knowledge, but it was a lie that she would not die. As a consequence of their disobedience, she and Adam became partakers of two kinds of death. The first is a physical death. Both Eve and Adam had possessed immortal bodies in the Garden of Eden. When they transgressed and were cast out, their bodies became mortal or subject to physical death. The second death was a spiritual death. Spiritual death occurs when we are separated from God, and it happened for Adam and Eve when they were cast out of God's presence. Believing it was the only way to acquire wisdom and knowledge, Eve had partaken (see Moses 4:9–12), and Adam, having committed himself to stay with Eve, also partook of the forbidden fruit. Adam and Eve and their posterity consequently became subject to physical death and were introduced into an environment of increased opposition where they could exercise their agency and acquire knowledge.

How does the Creation affect me daily? People can't exercise agency unless they are capable of making choices. A person can't make choices without encountering opposition. To have knowledge is to understand the full range of choices, and to exercise wisdom is to make a good choice.

Because of their limited experience (thus limited knowledge, limited opposition, and limited ability to exercise their agency), Adam and Eve could never be like God. They were too limited or ignorant. The Lord told Joseph Smith, "It is impossible for a man to be saved in ignorance"

(D&C 131:6). So we know that those three principles are key to our salvation. Every day I am on this earth I experience opposition, which gives me the opportunity to exercise my knowledge in making choices. Every day I hope my choices help me progress toward becoming like God (see 2 Nephi 2:11–19).

What does the Fall have to do with the plan of salvation? Eve gives us the answer in Moses 5:11: "Were it not for our transgression we never should have had seed, and never should have known good and evil, and the joy of our redemption, and the eternal life which God giveth unto all the obedient." Was this all a part of God's plan? Yes. Moses 4:6 says, "And [Satan] sought also to beguile Eve, for he knew not the mind of God, wherefore he sought to destroy the world." This scripture teaches us that God's purposes will never be frustrated (see also D&C 3:1–3). Eve explains that the Fall was necessary so that she and Adam could exercise agency and choose to have joy and children. In their state of innocence, Adam and Eve had neither joy nor sorrow (see 2 Nephi 2:11) because they did not have opposition. They also would have had no children until after the Fall (see 2 Nephi 2:23–25).

How does the Fall affect me daily? The scriptures tell us that while here on earth we are in a state of probation. We are exposed to wickedness and righteousness, misery and happiness, and other opposites. After experiencing happiness we can continue to make decisions to maintain that happiness and peace of mind or not (see 2 Nephi 2:21–24). One of the benefits of being separated from God is that no one is standing over our shoulder, pressuring us to choose God. We are free to make decisions and in this we can feel our agency in practice.

What does the Atonement have to do with the plan of salvation? Everything. The Atonement makes all of the aforementioned things possible. Without it we couldn't have opposition, agency, or knowledge. We would have only darkness and despair. Satan's plan did not include agency: "Behold, here am I, send me, I will be thy son, and I will redeem all mankind, that one soul shall not be lost, and surely I will do it; wherefore give me thine honor. . . . Satan rebelled against me [the Father], and sought to destroy the agency of man" (Moses 4:1–3). Satan wanted to control, dominate, and oppress us all.

How does the Atonement affect me daily? The answer to this is one of the most profound truths of the gospel. The Book of Mormon teaches that if there had been no infinite sacrifice made, Satan would be our ruler.

We can only imagine the misery that would be involved were we to be in Satan's power: "For behold, if the flesh should rise no more our spirits must become subject to that angel who fell from before the presence of the Eternal God, and became the devil, to rise no more. And our spirits must have become like unto him, and we become devils, angels to a devil, to be shut out from the presence of our God, and to remain with the father of lies, in misery, like unto himself; yea, to that being who beguiled our first parents, who transformeth himself nigh unto an angel of light, and stirreth up the children of men unto secret combinations of murder and all manner of secret works of darkness" (2 Nephi 9:8–9).

The joy of it all is that because of what Christ endured, we needn't succumb to fear and darkness. Rather, we can have happiness, joy, pleasure, and best of all, peace, because we are the beneficiaries of the Atonement Christ so lovingly provided. More amazing still is the fact that everyone has access to these gifts. Everyone who ever lived on this earth will ultimately be resurrected. Thus, death will be eliminated. People who love the Savior and appreciate what he has done for them, people who know of Christ but don't care that he suffered, people who aren't sure he really even existed, and those who have never heard of him will all receive the gift of immortality. All

God's children benefit, because he loves us all. Additionally, those who love the Savior and strive to keep his commandments can be redeemed from sin, cleansed, and made candidates for eternal life. All of this because of the Atonement. Does that affect me daily? Yes. And it will affect me throughout eternity as well. Because of that understanding, I may not always have happiness and joy, but I will always have peace—a gift from the Savior and Redeemer of the world.

The Son of God has perfect integrity. So much was his promise worth before the foundation of this world, that the salvation of all the earth's inhabitants rested upon his word. I find it impossible to place my faith anywhere else. I also find it impossible to not place my loyalty, my devotion, my trust, my love, and ultimately myself in his care. Experience has taught me that he does a far superior job with my life than I do. C. S. Lewis stated: "The Christian way is different: harder, and easier. Christ says, 'Give me all. I don't want so much of your time and so much of your money and so much of your work: I want You. I have not come to torment your natural self, but to kill it. No half-measures are any good. I don't want to cut off a branch here and a branch there [see Alma 22:15–18], I want the whole tree down. I don't want to drill the tooth, or crown it or stop it, but to have it out. Hand over the whole natural self, all the desires which you think innocent as well as the ones you think wicked—the whole outfit. I will give you a new self instead. In fact, I will give you Myself: my own will shall become yours' [see Alma 5:7, 14]" (*Mere Christianity* [New York: Macmillan, 1978], p. 167).

My Savior hasn't asked me to die for him. He has asked me to live for him, to live up to what he expects of me. I know his goal is that of the Father's: for me to return to him unashamed and with gratitude for the choice. That is my goal as well.

Stace Hucks Christianson served a mission to Holbrook, Arizona, and later taught seminary and institute for six years. She currently teaches at Brigham Young University and is working toward a master's degree in gender issues. She and her husband, Frank, have one child.

5

I LOVE THE BOOK OF MORMON!

Sue Egan

I love the Book of Mormon and know that it is true! As I daily read from its pages, the Spirit of the Lord fills my heart. Like Nephi of old, I too delight "in the scriptures, . . . and my heart pondereth continually upon the things which I have seen and heard" (2 Nephi 4:15–16).

Latter-day prophets have admonished us again and again to read and reread the Book of Mormon. President Ezra Taft Benson counseled us, "Now, my beloved brethren and sisters, let us read the Book of Mormon and be convinced that Jesus is the Christ. Let us continually reread the Book of Mormon so that we might more fully come to Christ, be committed to Him, centered in Him, and consumed in Him" (*Ensign,* November 1987, p. 85).

Great blessings and sacred promises have been pronounced upon the heads of each of us who follow the counsel to "flood the earth" with the book (see Moses 7:62; also see Ezra Taft Benson, *The Teachings of Ezra Taft Benson* [Salt Lake City: Bookcraft, 1988], p. 115). Several years ago President Benson stated, "I bless you with increased understanding of the Book of Mormon. I promise you that from this moment forward, if we will daily sup from its pages and abide by its precepts, God will pour out on each child of Zion . . . a blessing hitherto unknown" (*Ensign,* May 1986, p. 78). The heavens are literally opened in our behalf!

Moroni pleads with each of us to read this sacred book, and "ponder it in [our] hearts" (Moroni 10:3). Most of us desire to do this. But every now and then, we need to renew our efforts to make the Book of Mormon a part of our lives. For the past few years I have been compiling ideas that encourage Book of Mormon study. As I have shared these thoughts with youth across the country, they have in turn shared their favorite study methods with me. Every year the list continues to grow. Here are some of my favorites. Perhaps a few of them will appeal to you as you daily search the Book of Mormon: Another Testament of Jesus Christ.

1. Pray before you study, and invite the Spirit to be with you.

2. Choose one scripture from your daily reading. Write that verse in your journal and apply it throughout the day. This is one of the most powerful things you can do in your scripture study. Making the doctrine a part of your daily behavior fills you with the Spirit and purifies your life.

3. Use an inexpensive copy of the Book of Mormon. Use the "stop, ponder, and personalize approach." After reading a few verses, stop and ask yourself, "What is being said here? How does that apply to me in my life?" Make as many notations as you like in the margins. Put question marks next to things that you don't understand, then search for the answer. If a scripture reminds you of a personal experience, write some key words in the margin that will bring that event to mind. These markings will become a written testimony of how certain doctrines have affected you personally.

You can literally fill your scripture margins when using this method. That's why using an inexpensive copy of the Book of Mormon is ideal. You can write as many comments as desired without worrying about taking up limited space in your permanent scriptures. You can always transfer especially meaningful comments to your regular scriptures.

4. Insert your own name in the scriptures. For example, 1 Nephi 3:7 would read, "I (*insert your own name here*) will go and do the things which the Lord hath commanded, for I (*insert your own name here*) know that the Lord giveth no commandments unto the children of men, save he shall prepare a way for them that they may accomplish the thing which he commandeth them."

5. As you read the scriptures, look for principles that are being taught. In as few words as possible, summarize those principles in the margins. A chapter heading often includes principles that are contained in that chapter.

6. Memorize your favorite verses. One of my favorite EFY counselors, Lynette Willie, has memorized more than 450 verses!

7. Find a topic that interests you. Look it up in the Topical Guide. Then do one of two things:

a. Read all the words under that heading, omitting the references.

b. Look up every Book of Mormon reference under that heading.

8. Read through the Book of Mormon, highlighting all the various names of the Savior. (There are more than a hundred names.) Each of these names has a distinctive meaning.

9. Highlight every verse in the Book of Mormon that pertains to the Savior. I make a small colored dot next to the beginning of each verse that falls into this category. More than half of the verses in my Book of Mormon are marked with these dots.

10. Record your favorite verses on the blank pages located inside the cover sheets of your scriptures.

11. Read a verse or a chapter several times. This helps

you see details that you may not have noticed at first. Look up all the footnotes. Ponder the meaning of the verse again. Chances are, the more times you read the passage, the better you will understand it.

12. Read a chapter. Then, in your journal, paraphrase what that chapter says. Some choose to do this in their regular journals. Others prefer to keep a separate scripture journal.

13. Study selected chapters in the Book of Mormon. In your own words, teach the content of those chapters to a younger child. Learning doctrines well enough to teach them in a simplified manner increases your understanding.

14. Write the key words to a powerful scripture across the entire page. Wouldn't it be easier to find the story of Lehi's dream if the words "iron rod" were written in three-inch letters from margin to margin?

15. My friend Marge Kesler carries a supply of sticky notes inside the cover of her scriptures and records quotes from talks and articles on them. She then places the sticky notes next to appropriate scriptures for future reference.

This is helpful for two reasons. First, if you are not sure that you would like to keep that quote permanently in your scriptures, you can easily remove it later on. Also, quotes that are too lengthy to fit into the margin of your scriptures will often fit on one or two sticky notes.

16. Use the manuals that are available at the Church distribution centers. The Book of Mormon Student Manual for Religion 121 and 122 is especially helpful. It is full of quotes from the Brethren that will add to your understanding of the Book of Mormon. Copy your favorite quotes in the margin of your scriptures. When you write a quote in your scriptures, document not only who said it, but when (for example: President Benson, April conference, 1986).

17. One family set a goal to read through the Book of Mormon as many times as they could while their brother

was serving a mission. The parents bought a stack of inexpensive copies of the Book of Mormon and gave one to each child. As a family member finished reading his or her copy, that person would write a testimony inside the front cover and send the copy of the Book of Mormon to the missionary brother to give to an investigator. One young man sent his brother six copies in eighteen months!

18. Color selected scriptures according to topic. If a scripture contains more than one topic, the verse can be marked in one color and outlined in another. It is helpful to have a master key in front of your scriptures that describes what each color stands for.

19. One young woman keeps a small, spiral-bound notebook next to her scriptures. When she comes across a favorite verse she writes it in her notebook, recording just one scripture on each page. When all the pages are filled up, she then turns her notebook into a "scripture-a-day" book. She places the book on her dresser. Each day she turns to a new page and instantly has a new, favorite scripture to apply in her life.

20. Include objects in your scriptures. One girl placed a real mustard seed next to Matthew 13:31. She also put foil stars around Abraham 3:2. The possibilities are endless.

21. See how many days you can read from the Book of Mormon without missing a day.

22. If you hear an especially important talk at conference, make a reduced-size copy of it and keep it in your scriptures. One young woman carries President Benson's talk "Beware of Pride" (*Ensign,* May 1989, pp. 4–7) pasted inside the cover of her Book of Mormon.

23. Keep a copy of your scriptures next to your bed, so they will be nearby when you awaken and fall asleep.

24. Read the Book of Mormon from cover to cover, looking for just one topic. Color all scriptures that apply to that subject. (The Young Women values and their corresponding colors work well using this method.) In the front of

your scriptures, record the date you started and the date you finished searching for that topic.

Using an inexpensive copy of the Book of Mormon is ideal when doing this. Quite often I will use one copy five or six times to search for various topics. When most of the book is colored in, I place it in a special spot in my study and begin using another copy. (Give these copies away as the Spirit directs you.)

25. To find a favorite verse easily, write the key words that describe that verse in giant letters in the margin. Slightly wrinkle up that page and then flatten it out again. This makes the book fall open to that page more easily. One young woman told me that she puts baby powder on those pages to enhance the effect.

26. Carry a few pages of the Book of Mormon with you to study throughout the day. Some Latter-day Saint bookstores carry the Book of Mormon in single sheet form. This format is helpful when it isn't convenient to carry the entire book.

27. As you read through the Book of Mormon, make a genealogy-timeline chart. As new characters or civilizations come in, add them to your genealogy-timeline. Do this in pencil initially; later you can copy it in ink. (When I did this, I drew my chart going from top to bottom rather than from left to right. Trust me, you'll need to tape several pieces of paper together for this one.)

28. One young woman made a reduced-size copy of her patriarchal blessing. She laminated it and uses it as a bookmark in her Book of Mormon. Whenever she comes across a scripture that pertains to her patriarchal blessing, she colors that verse in yellow and puts the initials "pb" next to it.

29. Find a scripture study-buddy and set aside one time each week to study together. When my friend Karen and I did this, we studied five chapters a week from the Book of Mormon. We alternated being the "teacher." Although

both of us would independently study that week's reading assignment, it was the "teacher's" job to type up notes and commentary on that week's chapters and make a copy of those notes for each of us that we could refer to during our study time together. Before long, we had quite a lengthy collection of personal commentary and discussion notes in our special Book of Mormon notebooks.

30. Keep a small file box and index cards within reach as you study. When you come across a favorite scripture, write it on an index card and place it in the box. Before long you'll have a substantial file full of your favorite scriptures. Choose one card a day to implement and/or memorize.

31. Memorize, or at least become familiar with, definitions in the Bible Dictionary explaining principles that are often repeated in the scriptures. For instance, the word *grace* is discussed more than twenty-five times in the Book of Mormon. These verses are much more meaningful when we have a good understanding of the doctrine of grace. The same principle applies to dozens of gospel concepts.

32. Have a special, inexpensive, general conference copy of the Book of Mormon. Put the dates of the conference inside the front cover. Record notes from the talks in the blank pages inside the cover. Mark all the scriptures that the speakers refer to in their talks. In the margins, write ways that you can apply those principles. (This can be done in your regular scriptures if you have room.)

33. Memorize the Primary song "The Books in the Book of Mormon." This may help you find a certain book in your scriptures more quickly. At the very least, it makes your scripture study time more melodic!

34. Another favorite EFY counselor, Anna Nelson, told me that when a friend shares a favorite scripture with her, she puts her friend's name next to that verse. Then she writes a key word or two next to the scripture to remind her when and why that person shared it.

35. Read the Book of Mormon from cover to cover in thirty days. (That's about eighteen pages a day.) Reading it in such a short period of time allows you to see themes that you never noticed before. One year I did this each month for twelve months. That was an incredible experience!

36. One young man signs his name and records the date inside the cover each time he finishes reading the entire Book of Mormon. What a great idea! I can't think of a better thing to endorse with my signature than the Book of Mormon.

I hope you have found a few new study methods here that will enhance your feast upon the scriptures (see 2 Nephi 32:3; Alma 32:42). But remember, spiritual knowledge is not achieved merely with methods. Elder Richard G. Scott has told us, "Gaining spiritual knowledge is not a mechanical process. It is a sacred privilege based upon spiritual law" (*Ensign,* November 1993, p. 88). Spiritual knowledge comes as we humbly and earnestly seek to understand and live the doctrines of the gospel of Jesus Christ. The Book of Mormon will begin to change your life only when the Holy Ghost enters "in your mind and in your heart" and reveals eternal truths, and when you begin to incorporate those truths into your behavior (see D&C 8:2).

I testify from personal experience that great blessings have been unfolded to me as I have searched the Book of Mormon and applied its teachings in my life. These blessings are available to each of us. Our beloved prophet, Gordon B. Hinckley, has promised us that when we read the Book of Mormon, "There will come into your lives and into your homes an added measure of the Spirit of the Lord, a strengthened resolution to walk in obedience to his commandments, and a stronger testimony of the living reality of the Son of God, which promise I solemnly make in his holy name, even the name of Jesus Christ" (*Ensign,* November 1979, p. 9).

Sue Egan is a homemaker from Salt Lake City, Utah, and has served in a variety of Church callings, including Primary president, ward and stake Young Women president, and Primary music leader. She loves reading the scriptures and sharing the gospel. Sue and her husband, Rick, have six children.

6

THE ANCHOR OF HOPE IN CHRIST

Mark Ellison

Tell me about a discouraging experience you've had," I said to my seminary students.

One girl said, "My boyfriend broke up with me, then he took my sister out that same night."

The whole class groaned, and then a witty classmate quipped, "Look on the bright side—at least he stayed in the family!"

A young man in class told us, "I got in a wreck and chewed out the other guy. Then I went to pick up my date later that night, and her dad was the other guy." Gulp. What do you say at a time like that? Probably not, "Hey, fancy running into you again!"

A healthy sense of humor can help us deal with some disappointments, but not all of life's difficulties are so easily laughed off. Sitting among my students who are having dating problems are others who face more severe trials—the death of loved ones, divorce and family breakup, loved ones who are going astray, violence, depression, addictions, the weight of unrepented sin. For those who bear such heavy burdens, for all of us, the gospel of Jesus Christ has something glorious to give: hope.

Hope is a spiritual gift that fights off discouragement. It

is more than the wistful feeling someone has when saying, "I hope he asks me to Homecoming," or, "I hope I make the soccer team." Hope in a gospel sense is stronger than that. *Hope* is defined in dictionaries with words like *confidence, expectation,* and *trust.* In the scriptures, hope is often symbolized by an anchor (see Hebrews 6:19; Ether 12:4). Just as a ship in rough seas needs an anchor to keep it from going off course, we need to be anchored with confidence in Christ about the realities of this life and the next. "Wherefore, whoso believeth in God might with surety hope for a better world, yea, even a place at the right hand of God, which hope cometh of faith, maketh an anchor to the souls of men, which would make them sure and steadfast, always abounding in good works, being led to glorify God" (Ether 12:4).

One day, a seminary student of mine read to her class a poem she had written. With her permission, I share it with you as an example of how one's belief in God can be a stabilizing anchor, giving strength to endure life's trials:

> *On a lonely hill I stood alone*
> *Against a mourning sky,*
> *In a grief-filled world I'd never known,*
> *With none to hear my cry.*
>
> *Racked with pain, heart-broken, ill,*
> *I stood alone with my loss,*
> *Till it seemed I saw another hill,*
> *And a man on a cruel cross.*
>
> *He too had stood on a lonely hill*
> *In pain that would not cease,*
> *And I heard him say, "My child, be still,*
> *I give to you my peace.*
>
> *"Not as the world gives, do I give—*
> *The world may not understand—*
> *But I say unto you that you can live*
> *With this grief—if you take my hand."*

I came down out of the lonely hill,
And my sorrow found release—
My hand in his, my will his will,
And in my heart his peace.
—by Gina Harmer

As you read and ponder those lines, can you see that having hope is more than just being chipper? "Hope is always centered in Christ," Elder Bruce R. McConkie wrote (*Mormon Doctrine*, 2d ed. [Salt Lake City: Bookcraft, 1966], p. 365). Because of that, having hope is much more than what is called having a "positive mental attitude." It was Jesus who said, "Peace I leave with you, my peace I give unto you; not as the world giveth, give I unto you. Let not your heart be troubled, neither let it be afraid" (John 14:27).

In times of stress, I think there is a difference between the thoughts of someone whose hope is Christ-centered and those of someone who is merely trying to maintain a positive attitude.

POSITIVE ATTITUDE	HOPE CENTERED IN CHRIST
"Things will probably get better."	"If I 'watch and pray always,' things will never get worse than I can handle with the Lord's help" (see 1 Corinthians 10:13; Alma 13:28).
"I am strong enough to handle this."	"I can do all things through Christ which strengtheneth me" (Philippians 4:13; see also Alma 26:12).

Let me tell you about a modern-day example of being "anchored" in Christ. In February of 1993, President Howard W. Hunter, then President of the Quorum of the Twelve Apostles, came to BYU to speak at a fireside. Just as he stood to speak, a terrorist charged the pulpit and held up what he said was a bomb. The next few minutes were terrifying as 20,000 students and one prophet of God were held hostage. Some students cried out; others nervously began to sing a hymn. President Hunter held his place at the pulpit and said nothing. In the words of Elder Boyd K. Packer, President Hunter "just stood and looked on as if to say, 'When you are through, I'd like to go on with my talk'" (*Ensign*, April 1995, p. 29).

A distraction allowed the terrorist to be wrestled to the ground and taken away, and as soon as order was restored, President Hunter stood to address the shaken group of college students. His first words were a classic understatement: "Life has a fair number of challenges in it, and that's true of life in the 1990s."

He then delivered one of the most optimistic, cheerful messages I've ever known, full of faith and hope, and sprinkled with his grandfatherly wit and good humor. You ought to read the whole talk. Here's part of what he said:

> I am just a couple of years older than most of you, and in those few extra months I have seen a bit more of life than you have. I want you to know that there have always been some difficulties in mortal life, and there always will be. But knowing what we know, and living as we are supposed to live, there really is no place, no excuse, for pessimism and despair.
>
> In my lifetime I have seen two world wars, plus Korea, plus Vietnam and all that you are currently witnessing. I have worked my way through the Depression and managed to go to law school while starting a young family at the same time. I have seen stock markets and world economics go crazy, and I have seen a few despots and tyrants go crazy, all of which caused quite a bit of trouble around the world in the process.
>
> So I hope you won't believe all the world's difficulties have been wedged into your decade, or that things have never been worse than they are for you personally, or that they will never get better. I reassure you that things have been worse and they *will* always get better. They

always do—especially when we live and love the gospel of Jesus Christ and give it a chance to flourish in our lives (*Ensign,* October 1993, p. 70; see also *New Era,* January 1994, pp. 4–7).

We live in a time of many troubles, but also a time of righteous heroes like President Hunter. And better days are coming. In due time, there will be "a new heaven and a new earth," and "God shall wipe away all tears from [our] eyes; and there shall be no more death, neither sorrow, nor crying, neither shall there be any more pain" (Revelation 21:1, 4). In the words of the hymn that the BYU students sang that February night:

When dark clouds of trouble hang o'er us
And threaten our peace to destroy,
There is hope smiling brightly before us,
And we know that deliv'rance is nigh.
("We Thank Thee, O God, for a Prophet," Hymns, no. 19)

If you feel discouraged or hopeless at times, here's some advice: Read your scriptures! "For whatsoever things were written aforetime were written for our learning, that we through patience and comfort of the scriptures might have hope" (Romans 15:4). Over and over, the scriptures reassure us. One of my favorite verses, one that gives me comfort and peace, is 1 Corinthians 2:9: "Eye hath not seen, nor ear heard, neither have entered into the heart of man, the things which God hath prepared for them that love him." Thinking of that promise helps me remember: It's worth it . . . keep pressing forward!

Let me tell you a little about hope and repentance. Nothing destroys hope like unrepented sin, for sin always leads to despair (see Alma 41:10; *For the Strength of Youth,* p. 4). But nothing restores lost hope like turning to the Lord in humble, sincere repentance. "Whoso repenteth and cometh unto me as a little child, him will I receive" (3 Nephi 9:22).

One day a seminary student nervously asked me for help. "I've made some bad mistakes," she said, "and I want to repent. I know that I need to see my bishop as part of my repentance, but I'm afraid."

"What are you afraid of?" I asked.

"That my bishop will be angry. That he'll think I'm a disgusting person. Or that he'll tell my mom."

I tried to reassure her that the whole matter would be kept just between her, the bishop, and the Lord, and explained that the bishop is there as the servant of a loving Father in Heaven, not to condemn but to help people in their repentance. She took courage and decided to make an appointment to see her bishop.

"Hope is indeed the great incentive to repentance, for without it no one would make the difficult, extended effort required—especially when the sin is a major one" (Spencer W. Kimball, *The Miracle of Forgiveness* [Salt Lake City: Bookcraft, 1969], p. 340).

A few days later, my student approached me timidly, but with a bright smile. She seemed like a new person as she said, "I talked with my bishop last night, and it was so wonderful! He was kind and helpful. He explained so many things to me. I have a lot of changing to do, and we are meeting again in two weeks, but I feel so happy. There's hope for me!"

Among the changes that repentance brings is a feeling of comfort with the Lord. You feel happy to know he is there. You look forward to being with him someday. This young lady later wrote me a note, which she said I could share with others: "If I could give advice to anyone in my situation, I would just say to do it. Go talk to the bishop. It's so worth it. Before, I felt like I didn't belong in church, and I didn't feel like Heavenly Father would want to hear from me. But now, I feel like I can pray at any time, anywhere. And I love to attend church. Heavenly Father loves us, he can help us with anything."

Her experience reminds me of Alma the Younger, who described the effect of his repentance in a similar way. While in his sins, Alma felt "inexpressible horror" at "the very thought of coming into the presence of [his] God," but after repenting, his "soul did long to be there" with his Father in Heaven (see Alma 36:14–22).

A good measure of your hope might be, how would you feel about coming into the presence of God, right now? Alma himself asked us to consider that possibility: "Could ye say, if ye were called to die at this time, within yourselves, that ye have been sufficiently humble? That your garments have been cleansed and made white through the blood of Christ, who will come to redeem his people from their sins?" (Alma 5:27).

This scripture has become very meaningful to me because of an experience I had a few summers ago. I was training for the Utah Summer Games triathlon. One afternoon about five days before the race, I was out on my bicycle on a long training ride. I was excited, feeling good and strong, with hardly a care in the world. Suddenly, I felt a tremendous jolt, and then I was flying through the air. I had been struck from behind by a car that had swerved momentarily. It had hit me at about 55 miles per hour. My body skidded and tumbled until finally I was lying on my back on the side of the road. I was taken to the hospital, where doctors treated some painful injuries, including a broken leg and a lot of gravel that had become embedded in my arms, legs, and back. It would be a long time before I'd be able to race again.

At first, I felt angry about the driver who had been so careless, disappointed about my ruined summer of racing, and ashamed for not being very grateful that the worst I had suffered was a broken leg. Then a friend told me of a similar accident he'd seen reported on the news. Another vehicle, also going 55 miles per hour, had swerved over and struck two cyclists. The riders had been thrown more than 200 feet, and both were killed instantly. Finally, I saw how much there was to be grateful for. I am so thankful for life, for the chance to still be here to share earth life with my wife and wonderful children! I almost lost that.

I realized an important truth: You and I have no guarantee of how much time we have in this life. We have no assurance that we will still be here in fifty years, or five years, or even five hours. We have now, right now, in which to turn our hearts and our lives to the Lord (see Alma 34:32–34). And so, as Alma asked, are we ready, right now?

If we live properly every day, we can die any day. We can live with the same confidence Enos had, who said: "I rejoice in the day when my mortal shall put on immortality, and shall stand before him; then shall I see his face with pleasure, and he will say unto me: Come unto me, ye blessed, there is a place prepared for you in the mansions of my Father" (Enos 1:27).

Now, don't misunderstand; when Alma asked if we are ready, he wasn't asking if we are perfect. He asked, in a way, if we are headed in the right direction, if the atonement of Christ is cleansing us from our sins because we are humbly following Him.

Perhaps you, like me, sometimes feel the pangs of knowing that you fall far short of the perfect example of Christ you are trying to follow. I think there is a difference between this feeling and the pain experienced by a person who is not trying to follow Christ. The one who is trying feels spiritual urgings to do better in his or her forward progress; the other feels the alienation and frustration that are consequences of sin. The atonement of Christ brings hope to those who are trying: "And what is it that ye shall hope for? Behold I say unto you that ye shall have hope through the atonement of Christ and the power of his resurrection, to be raised unto life eternal" (Moroni 7:41).

Have you been baptized? Do you keep the covenant

alive by continually trying to live worthy of the Holy Spirit's companionship? If so, there is hope for you: You are on "the strait and narrow path." What remains is to keep pressing forward with a brightness of hope, and the promise is, "Ye shall have eternal life" (see 2 Nephi 31:17–20). What a wonderful reunion it will be when we are there at last!

As President Ezra Taft Benson wrote: "We must not lose hope. Hope is an anchor to the souls of men. Satan would have us cast away the anchor. In this way he can bring discouragement and surrender. But we must not lose hope. The Lord is pleased with every effort, even the tiny, daily ones in which we strive to be more like Him. Though we may see that we have far to go on the road to perfection, we must not give up hope" (*Teachings of Ezra Taft Benson* [Salt Lake City: Bookcraft, 1988], p. 398).

Mark Ellison teaches seminary in Springville, Utah, and serves as a counselor in a bishopric. He served a mission to the deaf and later taught American Sign Language at the Missionary Training Center and at Brigham Young University. Mark holds a bachelor's degree from BYU in English and is pursuing a master's degree in educational leadership. He and his wife, Lauren, have three children.

7

THE RULES OF ENGAGEMENT

Curt Galke

I strained to see the green illuminated lights on my alarm clock. Time was moving so slowly. At three in the morning the minutes dragged on as though they were hours. I must have been awake most of the night, tossing and turning. My mind could focus on only one image, that of being strapped into the backseat of an F-16 fighter, racing down the runway with full afterburners, the acceleration pressing me deep into the seat. I had waited my whole life for this experience, and I was sure that seven o'clock would never arrive. I love to fly almost as much as I enjoy breathing. When I joined the Air Force my ultimate dream was to fly in an F-16 fighter, and now only four hours stood in the way of having that dream come true.

The alarm startled me when it finally went off. I bolted out of bed, slipped into my flight suit, and rushed out of the house. Hurriedly I rode my bike through the mist of a typically humid Panamanian morning. We lived on the Air Force base, close enough to the flight line that I could hear every airplane take off and land. Minutes later I walked into the briefing room. Aerial maps of Central and South America dotted the walls, interspersed with pictures of military aircraft and squadron patches. Air crew bustled around the room getting ready for our mission. I couldn't help wondering which one of them was to be my pilot. A young captain approached and asked me if I was the doctor they were going to take along that day. Of course I was; who else in that room was walking four feet off the floor? He introduced himself as the pilot of our fighter and began the preflight briefing with those in the room.

Although we were embarking on a simple training mission using only two F-16s, the plans, emergency procedures, and rules of engagement had to be perfectly clear. By regulation, aircraft never leave the ground without a detailed briefing. When high performance fighters are darting around the sky at hundreds of miles per hour, there is no room for misunderstanding or mistakes. Altitudes, speeds, directions, coordinates—I was lost from the start. The briefing seemed to last forever, and I began to get restless. I was ready to strap on my parachute and survival kit, attach myself to the ejection seat, and fly! My frustration was obvious. On the walk out to the plane, my pilot commented, "Doc, all that technical talk must have been pretty boring for you. People who don't fly all the time don't understand how crucial those briefings are." He continued by relating the following story, which focused my attention on the need for rules of engagement.

On an unusually warm fall afternoon, two F-15 fighters were training high above the Nevada desert. Each pilot knew the importance of memorizing and practicing his combat maneuvers with precision. In a matter of weeks they would be flying aircraft in a desert war zone certain to be filled with enemy fire. Just prior to their training mission, they also had met to discuss and clarify the rules of engagement, in order to minimize any unnecessary risk and maximize the safety of an already dangerous mission.

The two experienced pilots took turns pretending to be the enemy screeching across the sky trying to gain a combat advantage. They would climb and then dive, bank

right and then left. The pursuing pilot would lock his mis-
siles onto the other aircraft; sensing the threat, the pilot
being pursued would climb almost vertically, attempting
to outmaneuver his "enemy." All was going as scheduled
and a valuable training exercise was almost over when one
of the jets disappeared. The remaining pilot searched the
sky frantically. In a dogfight, surprise is a friend only if it
is on your side. Suddenly the lost F-15 reappeared, but
something was terribly wrong. The incoming fighter was
on a direct collision course with the other jet. A quick eva-
sive maneuver proved not to be enough to avoid the collision. The impact crippled both jets; one spiraled quickly to
the desert below, where it exploded on impact. The surviving F-15 returned to home base, and the stunned pilot
reported the accident.

How could this have happened to two experienced
pilots who understood and had been trained to abide by
the rules of engagement? An Air Force officer who was
assigned to determine the exact cause of the accident inves-
tigated the crash carefully, recreating every detail of the
mishap. The investigator had the surviving pilot get into
the cockpit of his fighter, and while on the ground they
went through every move and every thought leading up to
the accident. Still no breakthrough. The investigating officer asked a few final questions, and suddenly the answer
became clear. The rules of engagement had not been followed. In the heat of battle, assigned flight altitudes had
been ignored. One of the jets was a thousand feet lower
than it was supposed to be, and the result was a midair collision that had cost an aviator his life. As the surviving
pilot got out of the F-15, he commented to the investigator,
"You know, when you're in the heat of the battle, sometimes you gotta throw out the rule book." What that sea-
soned pilot had failed to learn was that the rules of engagement are made to ensure a pilot's safety, *especially* in the
heat of battle.

"Each of us has his or her own battlefield. The tactics which the enemy will use against us will vary from time to time. He will seek to exploit our weak spots, so we must be alert to the devil's devious designs—the subtle sins and clever compromise as well as the obvious offenses" (Ezra Taft Benson, "In His Steps," an address given at the dedication of the Boise Institute of Religion, 20 November 1983, p. 1). Although the battles we fight every day may not seem to be as dramatic as a dogfight in a military jet, they are nevertheless very real and in a spiritual sense potentially just as deadly. We have been given a set of rules of engagement to guide us, even through the worst battles. Our safe return home depends on how well we know and apply those rules. The more familiar we are with the rules of engagement, the more likely we are to automatically follow them, especially in the most intense battles.

As the Savior's life was drawing to a close, he must have carefully chosen the instructions that he left his disciples. He would have wanted to make a lasting impression on their hearts and minds. Listen to the words of that simple sermon: "And this is life eternal, that they might know thee the only true God, and Jesus Christ, whom thou hast sent" (John 17:3). To know God and to apply his rules of engagement is the way to safely return to him. The Lord further taught us where we can find those rules: "Search the scriptures; for in them ye think ye have eternal life: and they are they which testify of me" (John 5:39).

I attended seminary, read the assigned scriptures, and memorized the scripture mastery passages. I outlined, colored, and even put a thin coat of varnish on the pages that contained what we used to call the scripture chase verses. When I opened my seminary scriptures many of the pages would "stand tall." I thought I really knew and understood those scriptures. Not until a wise MTC branch president, Elder Jay E. Jensen, focused my study of the scriptures did I really begin to feel the power that comes to those who search and apply the rules of engagement found therein. Let me share with you two keys that President Jensen taught me. They will open your eyes to the power of the scriptures.

1. We need to feast daily on the scriptures. Why do we spend more time watching TV than we do studying the scriptures? We have all probably used or at least heard the excuses, "I'm too busy," "They are so hard to understand," or "They're boring." Could the truth be that we just don't appreciate the value of what those pages contain? Here is key number one: focus on the promises contained in the scriptures. As you read particular verses, ask yourself, "What does this verse promise me if I will put forth the effort to study his word?" Hebrews 4:12 is a great example. "For the word of God [the scriptures] is quick, and power-ful, and sharper than any two-edged sword, piercing even to the dividing asunder of soul and spirit, and of the joints and marrow, and [the scriptures] is a discerner of the thoughts and intents of the heart."

The promise to us is that through regular scripture study we will be blessed with the ability to distinguish truth from error and to discern the thoughts and intents of others. The ability to do so is of inestimable value. For instance, we live in a world that would have us believe that one of God's greatest gifts to man, that of the powers of procreation, has little or no value beyond recreation. There are those in our society who are more concerned with a right to choose than a right to live. Friends tell us that a popular movie is rated R only because of its language and that we can't miss out on the best picture of the year simply because of its rat-ing. Commercials and advertisements bombard us every day with their idea of what is attractive and "cool." Teachers, books, movies, and friends constantly try to influence us to adopt their standards for what is true and right. Thank goodness Father has given us a means to discern truth from error! Discernment, or the ability to distinguish truth from error, is a marvelous gift given to those who wish to know and implement the rules of engagement.

Several years ago I had the opportunity to attend a testimony meeting that was held at the conclusion of a great youth conference in Oklahoma. I listened intently as some of those valiant youth wept while speaking of abusive and neglectful homes. Their stories tugged at my heart, and I felt a renewed gratitude for my own parents, who had raised me in an atmosphere of not only discipline but also love and respect. If you are a youth who has been touched by such an abusive or neglectful home, you might wonder how you could ever love and feel whole again. Is there a way to break the cycle of misery and mend the wounds? Carefully focus on the promise found in 1 Nephi 11:25, and you will have the answer. "And it came to pass that I beheld that the rod of iron, which my father had seen, was the word of God [the scriptures], which led to the fountain of living waters, or to the tree of life; which waters are a representation of the love of God; and I also beheld that the tree of life was a representation of the love of God." If you hold to the iron rod, or in other words, if you study the scriptures and apply them, the scriptures will lead you to the love of God. With that love you will be able to build comfortable, nurturing relationships.

Daily, each of us finds it necessary to approach our Father and ask forgiveness for mistakes and wrong choices. Some of our mistakes are of a more serious nature than others, but all of us have days when our soul just aches as we realize that our habits or perhaps even the friends we choose are keeping us from reaching our divine potential. There is power available to us through the rules of engagement, which will help us to repent of life's mistakes. Focus on the promise in Jacob 2:8: "And it supposeth me that they have come up hither to hear the pleasing word of God [the scriptures], yea, the word which healeth the wounded soul." Concentrated, daily scripture study can indeed soothe an aching heart as repentance heals the wounded soul.

2. The second key to bringing the scriptures to life is to understand that there is a price that must be paid in order to truly feel the power that comes from the written word. Just weeks after arriving in Panama, I went scuba diving with a friend of mine. We had chosen a secluded island for our dive, one that was accessible only by dugout canoe. As our families waited on the beach, my friend and I dove. For over an hour we swam around tropical reefs, chased colorful fish, and explored old shipwrecks. When we finally surfaced and tried to orient ourselves, we quickly saw we were in trouble. The current had been so strong that it had pulled us almost a mile offshore to a point where we couldn't even see the beach where we had started. The canoe that would return us to the mainland wasn't due back for two hours. As strong as the current was, I knew that in two hours we could be swept halfway to Colombia. A tropical storm was bearing down on us with heavy rain and strong winds, creating ocean swells that made swimming almost impossible.

We had only minutes of air left in our tanks, but we decided to dive to the bottom of the ocean where the current wasn't as strong and try to make our way back to the beach. We grabbed at rocks and coral as we pulled ourselves along the ocean floor for twenty minutes, before being forced to surface when our tanks ran out of air. We found that we had traveled far enough to at least see the beach, but we were dismayed to realize that the surface swim to the shore would be very long and strenuous. For almost an hour we swam the backstroke, the sidestroke, the breaststroke. For the first time in my life I was afraid of the water. I didn't want to die like this. The only thought I could focus on was of my wife and little boy back on the beach. No matter what it took, I was determined to make it back to them. The storm was intense, but slowly and ever so steadily, stroke by stroke, I was heading home. After what seemed an eternity of swimming we made it back to the safety of the beach and into the arms of our families. Every muscle in my body quivered from the strain. My shoulders were bleeding from where they had been rubbed raw by the weight of the air tank on my back. I had attained what I so desperately wanted, but only after I put forth an incredible effort and paid the required price.

The lesson is simple: if we desperately want the blessings, the counsel and advice that are available to us in the scriptures, we must be willing to do our part. Though the power contained in the scriptures is available to each of us, it isn't merely going to ooze out of the pages and take root in our hearts by our simply opening the books and reading. President Howard W. Hunter said, "Those who delve into the scriptural library, however, find that to understand requires more than casual reading or perusal—there must be concentrated study. It is certain that one who studies the scriptures every day accomplishes far more than one who devotes considerable time one day and then lets days go by before continuing. Not only should we study each day, but there should be a regular time set aside when we can concentrate without interference" (*Ensign*, November 1979, p. 64). A prophet has promised us the power of the scriptures if we are willing to pay the price to delve into a concentrated, daily study program.

I hope that you will deepen your commitment to become intimately acquainted with the scriptures. Therein you will find the rules of engagement that our Father has provided for your safe return to him. The scriptures contain the words of experienced, inspired prophets who spoke with God. They contain the answers to your questions and the solutions to your problems. The power contained in these books is yours if you are but willing to pay the price to search and study them.

* * * * *

The moment I had been waiting for was really here. My helmet and oxygen mask fit snugly, my G-suit was hooked into the aircraft, the ejection seat had been armed, and I was listening to our clearance instructions from the control tower. Glancing to my left, I noticed the other F-16 only feet from our wing tip preparing to take off in tandem with us. In a matter of minutes we would be airborne, playing tag with each other thousands of feet above the Panamanian jungle, traveling hundreds of miles per hour. How grateful I was for rules of engagement. A sense of security and peace came over me as I realized that these pilots had paid the price to learn the rules. I knew they would apply them that morning, even during the most intense minutes of our mission, and we would return safely home. The parking brake was released, the vibration and roar of the afterburner was deafening, and the force of acceleration pushed me deep into my seat as we rocketed down the runway.

Curt Galke served a mission in Mexico City and later taught Spanish at the Missionary Training Center. A graduate of Brigham Young University, he attended medical school in California and is now a third-year family practice resident in the United States Air Force. His goal is to become a flight surgeon. Curt and his wife, Alethea, are expecting their first child.

8

"HE CALLETH HIS OWN SHEEP BY NAME"

Cindy Bishop Grace

Recently, while reading the parable of the Good Shepherd in the New Testament, I was reminded of an experience that I had as a participant in a study abroad program in Israel. One autumn evening, my roommates and I were making plans for the following day. We had heard about an early morning sheep market, and some of the girls wanted to go see it.

"You're kidding, right?" I immediately questioned.

"C'mon. It'll be worth it once you're there," my friends replied.

"Very little is worth waking up before dawn," I argued.

"And as an added bonus, we can watch the sun rise over Jerusalem while we're walking. It will be beautiful!" they countered.

Despite my skepticism, my eager roommates finally talked me into going to the early morning sheep market. To a person who savors every last second under the covers, then scrambles to get dressed on time, waking up at 5:00 A.M. to watch a bunch of sheep being sold seemed next to ludicrous. However, I knew that my four-month study abroad program was winding down, and I didn't want to miss even one single experience.

Shortly after my nineteenth birthday, I had stepped onto
a jet, committing to myself that I would not waste any time
in the Holy Land or return home with regrets over missed
opportunities. The morning we were to go to the sheep
market, that promise to myself outweighed my sleepiness.
I poked one foot out from under the rust-covered blanket
and onto the cold, flat carpet. Rather quickly, I got dressed
and found myself walking down the familiar hill toward
the "Old City." This is a section of Jerusalem where Jews,
Christians, and Muslims reside. That these diverse people
should be able to live together is unusual, given the politi-
cal and religious unrest in the country.

Although I had walked this street several times during
my stay in Jerusalem, everything looked different on this
particular morning. It's amazing how the sun can paint a
variety of landscape pictures depending on the time of day.
To my left, the trees and sage on the Mount of Olives had a
slight bluish tint, and the square stone houses to my right
were waiting for the sun to make its approaching appearance over the walls of the city. It was actually exhilarating
to be up that early, although I would never have admitted
that to my victorious friends. The last thing I needed on
that peaceful morning was a chorus of "I told you so's."

We rounded the final bend on our walk to the market
and were assailed by the pungent smells of the city. It's
funny, I've been home for more than six years now, and I
really miss those smells. They sort of grow on you after a
while—figuratively speaking, that is. Anyway, as we
neared our destination, I wondered why this place was
called a sheep market. It looked like anything but a market. The dusty area was not enclosed. There were just a
bunch of sheep and their shepherds milling about in the
open space.

I was beginning to wish I had stayed in bed, when two
young Arab children scrambled down the slope in front of
us. The boys were about five and seven years old, shoeless

and wearing shirts that didn't quite cover their bellies. In an attempt to herd their sheep down the hill and into the market, they were yelling Arabic commands at the top of their lungs and frantically waving sticks in the air. I tried not to laugh at their futility as I watched the sheep scatter in front of the determined but ineffective children. The entire flock ignored the boys' commands, and the sheep refused to be herded.

Then I heard a calm but firm adult voice from behind. There came the father of the boys and the shepherd of the flock. He called the sheep by name, and the sheep, upon hearing the gentle voice, came one by one back into the fold. This shepherd brought order out of chaos, but the thing that amazed me most was that the shepherd apparently knew each individual lamb, and the sheep obviously recognized the voice of their master.

That early morning experience at the sheep market brought me a whole new understanding of John chapter ten in the New Testament. Verses three and four read, "And the sheep hear his voice: and he calleth his own sheep *by name,* and leadeth them out. . . . and the sheep follow him: *for they know his voice"* (emphasis added). I know that Christ actually knows us by name. Yes, even though there are millions of people in the world, just as in a flock of hundreds of identical sheep, the shepherd knows them individually. It is our responsibility to learn to recognize his voice through praying, studying the scriptures, and following his example.

Praying is like phoning our heavenly home when we feel far away. There really can be two-way communication when we learn how to recognize answers to prayers. While trying to make important decisions, I've often thought how nice it would be to be told what to do. I used to wish for grand or dramatic answers to my prayers. Just as the shepherd spoke calmly to his flock, however, so answers to prayers generally come in a soft way. The sheep listened not to the loud and demanding commands of the boys at the sheep market but to the soft, familiar voice of their master. The more we practice patient listening, the more we learn to recognize the quiet promptings of the Spirit or the Shepherd.

Next, the scriptures are like letters written from our heavenly home. At the BYU Jerusalem Center we had what we fondly termed "the mail wall." The entire wall was filled with wooden slots, and each slot was assigned to a different student. Every afternoon we checked our slots, hoping for the slightest morsel of information from home. I don't come from a family of letter writers, so my daily search for mail was usually fruitless. However, one day I received a package. I remember feeling disappointed that Mom had scrawled only a few sentences: "How are you? It's snowing here. The kids built a snowman in the front yard. Hope all is well. Love, Mom." Feeling a little home-sick, I continued to open my package, which contained the new set of scriptures I'd been waiting for. Thumbing through the shiny gold-edged pages, I realized that the scriptures are like letters from our heavenly home. They contain detailed stories and information that Heavenly Father wants us to know. By studying the teachings of the prophets and the life of Christ, we learn to better recognize His voice in our lives. Along with prayer, scripture study provides us direct communication with our heavenly home.

Finally, we can follow the Savior's example and act as shepherds for others until we go home. At the priesthood session of general conference in April 1995, President James E. Faust gave an address entitled "Responsibilities of Shepherds." He related the following experience:

> When I was a very small boy, my father found a lamb all alone out in the desert. The herd of sheep to which its mother belonged had moved on, and somehow the lamb got separated from its mother, and the shepherd

must not have known that it was lost. Because it could not survive alone in the desert, my father picked it up and brought it home. To have left the lamb there would have meant certain death, either by falling prey to the coyotes or by starvation because it was so young that it still needed milk. Some sheepmen call these lambs "bummers." My father gave the lamb to me and I became its shepherd.

For several weeks I warmed cow's milk in a baby's bottle and fed the lamb. We became fast friends. I called him Nigh—why I don't remember. It began to grow. My lamb and I would play on the lawn. Sometimes we would lie together on the grass and I would lay my head on its soft, woolly side and look up at the blue sky and the white billowing clouds. I did not lock my lamb up during the day. It would not run away. It soon learned to eat grass. I could call my lamb from anywhere in the yard by just imitating as best I could the bleating sound of a sheep: *Baa. Baa.*

One night there came a terrible storm. I forgot to put my lamb in the barn that night as I should have done. I went to bed. My little friend was frightened in the storm and I could hear it bleating. I knew that I should help my pet, but I wanted to stay safe, warm, and dry in my bed. I didn't get up as I should have done. The next morning I went out to find my lamb dead. A dog had also heard its bleating cry and killed it. My heart was broken. I had not been a good shepherd or steward of that which my father had entrusted to me. My father said, "Son, couldn't I trust you to take care of just one lamb?" My father's remark hurt me more than losing my woolly friend. I resolved that day, as a little boy, that I would try never again to neglect my stewardship as a shepherd if I were ever placed in that position again. (*Ensign,* May 1995, p. 46)

Not all of us will be asked to care for a literal lamb. But there are people around us who would benefit from and even sometimes need our service or simple friendship.

When we begin treating others as Christ would, it becomes easier to recognize his voice and influence in our own lives.

Praying, studying the scriptures, and following the Savior's example are three ways we can learn to recognize the voice of the Shepherd. The scriptures tell us that while watching a flock, a *hireling* will run away if danger approaches. However, a *shepherd* will stay and fight for his sheep even unto death. Jesus Christ is the perfect example of the Good Shepherd, as is explained in John 10:11–15:

> I am the good shepherd: the good shepherd giveth his life for the sheep. But he that is an hireling, and not the shepherd, whose own the sheep are not, seeth the wolf coming, and leaveth the sheep, and fleeth: and the wolf catcheth them, and scattereth the sheep. The hireling fleeth, because he is an hireling, and careth not for the sheep. I am the good shepherd, and know my sheep, and am known of mine. As the Father knoweth me, even so know I the Father: and I lay down my life for the sheep.

Our Shepherd, the Savior Jesus Christ, sweated beads of blood and then laid down his life for us that we might escape the bonds of death and return to him someday. He loves us. He knows each of us by name. If we will learn to recognize and follow his voice, he will lead us home.

Cindy Bishop Grace teaches junior high drama, English, and communications. She has worked as an actress and as an EFY counselor and coordinator. This is her seventh year of involvement with EFY. Cindy studied in Israel for four months and has filled a Church service mission in Nauvoo, Illinois.

9

HIDDEN POCKETS, HIDDEN TALENTS, AND PROFITABLE SERVANTS

Kim Novas Gunnell

"Five-thirty in the morning!" Had I heard right? The bishop was extending a calling for me to teach early morning seminary. I didn't exactly know how to respond. "Are you seriously telling me I'll have to get up at 5:30 every morning?"

"No," the bishop assured me. I felt relieved.

"Seminary *starts* at 5:30. You'll have to be there at 5:00 to unlock the church and set up."

"Bishop, the church is ten miles from my house."

"I guess you'll have to leave about 4:40."

"But Bishop, it takes me a good hour to do my hair and makeup."

"I guess that means you'll be getting up at 3:30." I was numb. Was this really happening?

"So, will you do it?" the bishop asked.

I took a deep breath. Besides getting up early, I knew I would also be going to bed late because I would be studying harder than I ever had. I knew this would require sacrifices by my husband and children. I knew that this calling would be difficult. But I also knew that it came from the Lord. "Yes," I said, "I think this will be a great blessing."

And that's just what it was. I look back at teaching seminary in Nashville, Tennessee, as one of the highlights of my entire life. At first I was fearful. I didn't feel as though I was a scripture scholar. I didn't feel as though I could teach as well as others. I was worried that I wouldn't be able to relate to teenagers and that some of my students would eat me alive. As the year progressed, however, I found joy in studying the scriptures, and as I asked for the Spirit's guidance, I found I could teach effectively—on good days. I loved my students and they responded positively to me. That year in seminary I discovered some hidden talents I didn't even know I had, and I had the opportunity to develop them.

In the parable of the talents, Jesus told of a man who gave one servant five talents, another two, and another one. The man left for a season, and returned to find that the first two servants had doubled their talents. This pleased the master. However, the third servant had hidden his talent in the earth, and because he had done nothing to use or develop what his master had given him, the master was displeased (see Matthew 25:14–30). One obvious message of this parable seems to be that if we want to be considered profitable servants in our Master's eyes, we must discover our talents, have faith that Heavenly Father will help us develop them, have the courage to try, and then work hard and persevere.

Discover your hidden talents. Brother Jack Weyland tells about being asked to be a substitute teacher for an early morning seminary class. On the day he was to teach the class, he put on his brown suit, then went to drop his hairbrush in the side coat pocket, only to discover that the pocket was full of cookie crumbs. He had been at a wedding reception a few days earlier and decided he didn't like the cookie he was eating, so he had slipped it into his suit pocket and forgotten it was there.

Brother Weyland says, "You can't put a hairbrush into a pocket full of cookie crumbs, because if you do, after you brush your hair with it, people will think you have a very unusual form of brown dandruff." He tried to slip his brush into the other pocket of his suit, but that pocket was fake. Suddenly, Brother Weyland got angry at the idiot company that would design a suit with only one side pocket. He went to a drawer, got a pair of scissors, and attacked the fake pocket.

Brother Weyland continues, "Guess what? It wasn't a fake pocket after all. The manufacturer had sewn it shut, and for the past six years, all I needed to do was cut one piece of thread and I would have had two pockets instead of just one. The pocket had been available for the past six years, but because I didn't believe it was there, it sat . . . unused" (*If Talent Were Pizza, You'd Be a Supreme* [Salt Lake City: Deseret Book, 1986], pp. 18–19).

Like Brother Weyland, we all have hidden pockets— hidden pockets of talents just waiting to be discovered. Our Heavenly Father has given all of us gifts and talents (see D&C 46:11–12). In fact, President George Q. Cannon said: "We are the children of God, and as His children there is no attribute we ascribe to Him that we do not possess, though they may be dormant or in embryo" (*Gospel Truth* [Salt Lake City: Deseret Book, 1974], 1:1). Sometimes our pockets of talents are hidden and sewn shut, but they are there! We just have to find them.

Have faith. Frederick W. Babbel told of a valuable lesson he learned at the Grand Canyon when their guide showed them a twisted, gnarled, old juniper tree that was literally growing out of the side of the rock canyon wall. "How can it grow there?" Brother Babbel asked the guide.

The guide explained that a juniper seed is shaped like a cantaloupe seed. Apparently, one of these small seeds fell into a crevice near the edge of the canyon wall. Everything was solid rock. You would think that the seed would not possibly be able to germinate with no soil, little if any water, and virtually no sunshine down in the crevice. Yet the seed germinated, implanted roots into the solid rock, and grew.

Brother Babbel wrote: "As it continued to grow and expand into a full-fledged, though misshapen, tree, its trunk and its roots began to exert a continuing pressure on the outer ledge of rock. Finally the pressure became so great that one entire large section of the canyon wall broke loose and crumbled into a massive heap near the base of the canyon. . . . The guide said it was estimated that forty million tons of rock lay at the base of this tremendous canyon because that little seed didn't know it could not grow" (*To Him That Believeth* [Salt Lake City: Bookcraft, 1982], pp. 1–2).

That's the kind of faith each of us needs to have as we strive to discover our hidden talents and try to develop them.

Have the courage to try. Do you realize that some of our favorite songs that we sing in the Church were written by composers who at one point didn't think they could write music? Janice Kapp Perry grew up playing musical instruments, but never thought of writing music until one year when she was called to work with her ward roadshow. The stake leaders announced that wards could earn extra points if they used original music, so Sister Perry said, "Okay, I'll try."

Kenneth Cope always enjoyed singing, but didn't think he could write music until one summer when he was working as an EFY counselor and some of the leaders said, "Wouldn't it be great to have a theme song?" Kenneth said, "Well, I'll try." How grateful we all are that Sister Perry and Brother Cope were willing to try something new.

My brother-in-law, Brad Wilcox, says, "Trying is like

climbing a hill. If you stand with your feet firmly planted at the bottom and declare that there is no way you can climb that hill, you could stand there forever. If you dare to try, you have nowhere to go but up" (*The Super Baruba Success Book* [Salt Lake City: Bookcraft, 1979], p. 69).

Such advice may make trying sound easy, but it's usually not. Trying something new can be frightening. Remember Enoch in the scriptures? He was commanded by God to tell the people to repent. "And when Enoch had heard these words, he bowed himself to the earth, before the Lord, and spake before the Lord, saying: Why is it that I have found favor in thy sight, and am but a lad, and all the people hate me; for I am slow of speech; wherefore am I thy servant?" (Moses 6:31).

Wait, what's the problem here? Enoch was a prophet! He heard the voice of God! But even that didn't make it easy for him to find the courage to try. At times, all of us feel just as frightened and insecure. But God made a wonderful promise to Enoch that applies to us too: "And the Lord said unto Enoch: Go forth and do as I have commanded thee, and no man shall pierce thee. Open thy mouth, and it shall be filled, and I will give thee utterance, for all flesh is in my hands" (Moses 6:32).

Heavenly Father will not forsake any of us in our efforts toward self-betterment. As we discover our talents, have faith, and find the personal courage to try, he will support and bless us. So, paint that picture, try out for that play, learn to cut hair, sing the song, read the book, talk to your friends about the Church, compliment someone you admire.

Work hard and persevere. Although it's true that any journey begins with the first step, most journeys don't end there. As important as first steps are, they must be followed by lots and lots of other steps. Longfellow wrote, "The heights by great men reached and kept, were not attained by sudden flight; but they, while their companions slept, were toiling upwards in the night."

I've already shared how I was called to teach early morning seminary, but let me also share how I came to teach at EFY. I had spoken at firesides during college days as I had the opportunity to tour with the BYU Young Ambassadors and with the musical production *My Turn on Earth*. I always enjoyed speaking at firesides, but didn't feel like I was very effective. I felt much more comfortable singing before a group than speaking.

When I was first invited to apply to be part of the EFY faculty, I thought it was a mistake. My husband reminded me of a line in my patriarchal blessing in which I was told that it would be my great privilege to be a teacher to the youth of the Church. "Perhaps," I reasoned to myself, "this is one of those hidden pockets I haven't discovered yet."

I had faith that if this was something my Heavenly Father wanted me to do, I could do it even though at that point in my life I didn't see how. I felt much safer singing and acting because I was sharing the words, thoughts, and feelings of others. How would I ever be able to share my *own* feelings and thoughts in a way that might teach and motivate others? Still, I had faith that God could strengthen me, so I began to fill out the application that had been sent to me.

As I went through that process, I lost any courage I had mustered to that point. The application called for titles for not just one presentation, but *four*. I needed to provide main points, supporting points, and complete outlines with scripture references for *four* presentations. I had a hard time bearing my testimony in Church, let alone speaking for four hours. I'm embarrassed now to admit that the EFY faculty application forms sat on my desk for more than two years before I finally found the courage to try. After I finally completed them and sent them in, to my amazement, I was accepted!

My first assignment was at an EFY held in Indiana. As that first EFY approached, I prepared harder than I have for anything in my life. I wrote and rewrote my presentations so many times that my brain hurt. I practiced in front of the mirror, the dog, the empty living room, and even the dirty dishes in my kitchen sink. There I was, quoting scriptures to dirty dishes! I read every book on speaking I could get my hands on. I wrote out the main points and references for each of my presentations on little note cards. I was scared, but I was ready.

I went to Indiana and met the EFY teachers and counselors and the youth. I became more and more nervous as the hour of my first class approached. Another teacher, Randy Bird, realized how I was feeling and was kind enough to walk me to my assigned room. He offered some much-needed and much-appreciated encouragement and support. Soon the room began to fill with young people. I smiled, shook hands, and greeted some who sat in the front. Then I went to my purse to pull out my notes—my blood, sweat, and tears. The note cards weren't there. I shook the purse and looked again. I couldn't find them anywhere. Even the printed lyrics of the new song I had planned to sing weren't there. I couldn't possibly remember all those words! I panicked as I realized I must have left them in my room. But now it was time to start, so there was nothing for me to do but swallow hard and pray. I pleaded with God to bless me as he had blessed Enoch. I reminded Heavenly Father that I was there on his errand and that I had done all I could do to prepare. Now, I needed his help to bring the main points of my presentation, the scripture references, and the song lyrics to my remembrance.

That very first EFY experience in Indiana was actually a little miracle for me. I felt as if God whispered to me the same message he had given Enoch: "Open thy mouth, and it shall be filled, and I will give thee utterance" (Moses

6:32). That's exactly what happened. My talks had never gone so well in all the times I'd practiced them. I actually felt as if I did better and had better eye contact with the young people because I wasn't able to bury my head in my notes. When I sang my song, the words came to my mind as if someone were whispering them to me phrase by phrase.

The Lord had answered my desperate prayer. I had no choice but to rely totally on him, and he carried me through that experience. I opened my mouth and it was filled. Forgetting my notes was the best thing that ever happened to me. With this new confidence I vowed that, although I would prepare, I would try to deliver my presentations without notes, so I could look at the young people I was teaching.

Although I consider what happened in Indiana to be a miracle, I'm sure I wasn't nearly as polished as the speakers those youth were accustomed to hearing. I'm sure that most of the young people in that room for my first EFY presentation must have wondered who had ever invited me to come. I'm sure many other young people through the years have wondered the same thing. I don't really blame them. After all, I wonder the same thing myself every time I look at the list of who is teaching with me. But I'm trying. I'm hanging in there, persevering, and not giving up.

I discovered a hidden talent, had faith that Heavenly Father would help me, found the courage to try, and am now working hard to improve. Why? Because, just as in the New Testament parable, I want the Lord to be able to say to me, "Well done, thou good and faithful servant: thou hast been faithful over a few things, . . . enter thou into the joy of thy lord" (Matthew 25:21). Heavenly Father and Jesus Christ have given *all of us* so much. We must be willing to do all we can to become more profitable servants for them.

Kim Novas Gunnell holds a bachelor's degree in musical theater from Brigham Young University. She toured with the BYU Young Ambassadors for two years and was the 1993–94 Miss Utah U.S.A. She has taught early morning seminary and has been on the EFY faculty for six years. She and her husband, Doug, have three children.

10

JUST SAY NO TO STINKIN' THINKIN'

Suzanne Hansen

Have you ever heard anyone say . . .
"It wasn't my fault; I didn't hear my alarm."
"I couldn't get to my homework; I was too busy."
"The devil made me do it."
"It's *all* your problem. You're the one to blame!"
"I just can't do it!"
"I'm always late; I just can't help it."
"If only my parents understood."
"I don't have time."
"I'm just no good."
"I'm so depressed."
Well, frankly, all these comments are the result of "stinkin' thinkin'." Basically, "stinkin' thinkin'" keeps us in a rut, prevents us from taking responsibility for our own lives, and stops us from changing for the better.

But how can we sort out the "stinkin' thinkin'" from all the "stuff" we *have to* think about all day long? What about history class, English class, math, new computer programs, making the team, getting the car Friday night, and really important things like how to program the VCR so it will stop blinking 12:00? At the same time, you may be thinking about the latest fashion trends, TV shows, video releases, or your next date. You may also be keeping track of fat grams in that cheeseburger or studying the wrapper for contents of the junk food you just ate or worrying about how your dress is going to fit for the dance or agonizing over the big zit forming on the end of your nose.

Your mind may be filled with so much information, so many thoughts, facts, and concerns, that sometimes it may be hard even to get to sleep at night.

However, it's the "stinkin' thinkin'" that will do the damage in your life. And it's the attitude with which you view all the stuff in your life that will determine your peace of mind. As Dennis Deaton once said to me, "It's the set of the sail, and not the gale, that determines the way we go." Our thoughts powerfully determine our life's direction and what we accomplish.

Every one of the spectacular creations of humanity began as a thought or an idea. From the idea came the plan, from the plan came the action, and from the action came the object. Whatever you're sitting on or reclining in had its origin as someone's thought. Even the room you're in right now and everything in it, including the clothes you have on, began as a thought.

ALL CREATION COMES FROM THOUGHT

All the good, the great, the fine, the noble, and the creative acts of humanity were conceived in someone's mind. The Eiffel Tower, the *Declaration of Independence,* the Salt Lake Temple, the *Mona Lisa,* great movies, and all classic literature hatched from a thought. Even *you,* as the old saying goes, "began as a twinkle in your father's eye."

On the other hand, all the terrible conflicts and evil behavior in this world—fighting, lies, abuse, discrimination, and wars—began as a thought. Sure, Satan deserves a lot of the credit as the father of "stinkin' thinkin'," but we seem to come up with a lot of it on our own as well. Remember, our Father in Heaven can't help us unless our minds are purged of doubt and prepared to receive the influence of his Spirit. Thus, the scriptures counsel us, "As [a man] thinketh in his heart, so is he" (Proverbs 23:7).

Let's explore the advantages of thinking with our hearts—the kind of thinking that lifts us up instead of dragging us down, that invites the Spirit of the Lord instead of chasing it away.

THINK YOUR WAY OUT OF A RUT

You are the result of a lifetime of thinking. Are you pleased with what you see in your life? If you're not exactly ecstatic about the way things have gone so far—if you feel as though you're in a rut—then you may want to consider this simple solution: Change the way you think about what has happened to you. The good news is that, since you are in control of what you think about, you can change your life *immediately*, just by changing your thoughts. You will see later on how this can happen when I share with you the true story of David.

To get out of a rut, begin to think of your trials and challenges as blessings and teachers in your life, which will bring you closer to solutions and success. Thomas Edison's life is a great example of this principle. Many would have given up after failing 1,000 times in an attempt to create a workable light bulb. But Edison didn't quit after 2,000 failures or after 3,000. After 4,000 unsuccessful tries, he told his associates, "At least we know 4,000 ways it doesn't work, which brings us closer to the way it will work."

Finally, after 5,000 experiments, Edison was successful, and his invention literally *lit up the world*. Out of his creative thinking came also the phonograph, motion pictures, and an improved telephone, all because he refused to give up. He always looked for a better way and he *knew* he would eventually find it. And in hundreds of instances, he did. No ruts in Edison's life.

TAKING PERSONAL RESPONSIBILITY

Besides rescuing you from the ruts in your life, correct thinking from the heart will also help you understand who it is that is responsible for your ups and downs. It's you! The world is a tumultuous place, but have you noticed how some people seem to always land on their feet? That may be because they live by the principle, "If it is to be, it is up to me."

Vernon Howard tells a very interesting story about self-determination. He compares life to a ship that is battered by a storm and subsequently loses its rudder. Instead of repairing it, the crew members set up counseling sessions to calm the frightened passengers and to convince them that "the rudderless way is the natural way. Take advantage of the time, engage in shipboard activities, keep yourself busy."

However, one passenger, whom Mr. Howard calls *True Voyager*, notices that the ship is going in circles. Although he mentions this to the other passengers, they ridicule him for his notions and lack of faith in the program.

True Voyager then thinks that if he is to ever get off the rudderless ship, he will have to do something about it himself. He alone is responsible to see that he arrives at his destination. The next time he sights land in the ship's ever widening circle, he leaps overboard and swims to solid ground (see *The Power of Your Supermind* [Englewood Cliffs: Prentice Hall, 1975], p. 105).

Our Father in Heaven will not abandon us, even in a sea of trouble. He has given us the guidance of the Holy Ghost in all things. But first we have to ask for this help, prepare to receive the answer, and then take personal responsibility to act.

OUR THOUGHTS CAN LIMIT US

No amount of blaming others for our mistakes or problems will ever change our circumstances. Assigning blame only restricts our ability to find solutions or create options. It is also true that many people limit their own potential by continuing to embrace preconceived notions, much like trained elephants in India. There, a baby elephant is secured by a heavy chain that is attached to its leg and then to a stake driven deep into the ground. No matter how hard the young elephant tugs on the chain, it is unable to get away. Finally, it resigns itself to the fact that as long as it is attached to the stake, it cannot get away. As mighty adults, elephants trained in this way can be secured to a stake by only a small rope. Even though they possess the strength and potential to snap the rope easily with one swing of a leg, their conditioning keeps them prisoner.

A similar example of conditioning is described by Deepak Chopra. An experiment was conducted in which a very large aquarium was divided into halves by a glass partition. Fish were kept in one half of the tank and open water in the other. During the first week of the experiment the fish continually bumped into the glass divider while trying to swim through. After three weeks of conditioning, however, the fish learned to swim up to the divider without bumping into it.

Then an amazing thing was demonstrated. Even after the glass divider was removed, and the fish were free to swim the whole length of the aquarium, they would not swim past the point where the divider had been (see *The Higher Self,* an audio presentation [Simon & Schuster, 1993]).

People can also be conditioned, similar to these animals, to expect only certain things. Even though we possess superior abilities to reason and create, we are sometimes severely limited by our very strength—our ability to think.

Thoughts take many forms. Fear is perhaps the most debilitating.

To see David today, at age eighteen, no one would ever know that he had once been a very withdrawn, fearful boy.

Today, we see a tall, handsome Eagle Scout, a decorated athlete, an accomplished, award-winning artist. Seeing him now, no one would suspect that David had once trembled at the thought of trying *anything* for fear of failing. He had been required to repeat kindergarten and to take "special ed" classes all the way through grade school and junior high school.

What changed for David? First, he wanted to believe what loving parents were telling him—that he was a son of God with unlimited potential. He knew his parents believed in him; he now wanted to believe in himself. He was sixteen then, just finishing his sophomore year of high school.

Then his aunt gave him an audio tape. He has listened to it each day now for two years. The tape is about visualizing success—training one's mind to see a desirable outcome. Listening to the tape, David formulated a personal creed: "Hard Work Is Worth It!"

David began to visualize himself working hard and succeeding at everything he did. He had always loved to run—now he was about to find out how good he was. He went out for the track team, and he made it. By his senior year, David had become the anchor of the cross-country team. He visualized going to the state meet and doing very well. He placed among the top twenty finishers. And then his track coach paid him the supreme compliment.

Each year the coach gave out two awards at the end of the season: a huge trophy for the "Runner of the Year" and a coveted plaque, the "Eye of the Tiger" award for the team member who most exemplified devotion and hard work during the season. David was stunned to win both awards.

While David was excelling in track, he was also blossoming as an artist. By his senior year, David was doing such impressive work that his art teacher signed him up for art classes at the local college, classes he completed while he was still in high school. At Tulsa Technical

College, David entered an art competition, and his design for a wall mural was accepted. He had the honor of painting his mural on the side of a building on the college campus.

Then the boy who had been in "special ed" classes for nine years tackled his ACT tests with confidence. David scored higher than any of his older brothers and sisters before him. David now has a scholarship offer from Oklahoma State University.

NEW DIRECTIONS

There is a lesson for all of us in David's success. He learned that by changing his thoughts and beliefs about himself, he could completely change the direction of his life. His abilities had always been there, but now confident thinking replaced fear.

Spiritual thoughts can also change our life's direction. Soon after entering the Missionary Training Center as a new missionary, John reflected on how his priorities had changed and how his life had been enriched by a spiritual focus. He then wrote this poem, which he entitled simply "John":

> He worked out for years to reduce all his fat.
> His muscles were firm and his stomach was flat.
> He jogged night and morning to keep himself trim,
> And still found time to play racquetball and swim.
> He drank protein drinks, and ate health food galore,
> Then lifted, stair-climbed, and lifted some more.
> He told fam and friends that it gave him a "high."
> They said not a word as he waved them good-bye.
> "If things work out," he yelled back from afar,
> "I'll be a great athlete, I'll be a big star!"
> But, why could he not see the truck up ahead?
> One thud . . . and his beautiful body lay dead.
> And then he saw something that filled him with fright.
> His spiritual body was one sorry sight!
> A skeleton, covered with nothing but skin.

He got up to heaven, but didn't get in!
"Another soul's mine," Satan started to scream,
"Give man something nice, and he'll take the extreme!"
OK, I'll admit it; I'll outright confess.
For the fast way to hell, take the excess express.

Even good things in excess can be the result of "stinkin' thinkin'." Say no to it. Be emphatic. Say no to fear and lack of faith. They hold us back as surely as if we were being restrained by heavy chains. Be personally responsible for the course of your life.

As John later said in a letter written as he crossed the Atlantic Ocean on the way to his mission assignment in Europe: "The day I enlisted in God's army was the best day of my life!"

May we all enlist and turn our thoughts toward home— our home on high. If we will do that, our lives here on earth will be much better.

Suzanne Hansen is a lecturer and business-woman in Salt Lake City, Utah. She has worked as a newspaper columnist, appeared on TV talk shows, and authored five books. A former college homecoming queen, she enjoys arts and crafts, flower arranging, and classical and new age music. Suzanne and her husband, Michael, have three children.

II

THIS POSTCARD IS FOR YOU!

Victor W. Harris

During the spring and early summer of 1985, I had the wonderful opportunity, as one of Brigham Young University's Young Ambassadors, to travel to Egypt, Turkey, Jordan, and Greece on a seven-week show tour. During our tour, we performed at many ancient biblical and modern sites, learned a great deal about many cultures, and made many friends.

One of the friends we made was particularly precious. We met him in Egypt, in front of a papyrus shop located just outside of Cairo, not very far from the great pyramids. Our group had just come from a visit to the pyramids, where we had each had the experience of riding a camel. Many of us were still reeling from the culture shock created by the odors of that very foreign country, the stark desert landscape, and the discourteous behavior of the Egyptain vendors.

The moment we stepped off the bus at the pyramids, we were swarmed by a host of pushy men intent on selling us their wares. They made us extremely uncomfortable by their aggressive approach to us. We were eye to eye, face to face, and practically nose to nose with them as they shouted things like, "Ten postcards—one American

dollar!" and "Camel rides—only one dollar!" After endur-
ing a few minutes of that kind of sales tactics, many of us
felt like saying, "Here, take my money! I don't care if you
even give me anything back! Please, just leave me alone for
a few moments!"

After a short while most of us got used to the system
and entered into the bartering that typifies the Near East
way of doing business. Nearly all of us paid to take a ride
on a camel. It was a unique experience to sit on one of
those tall beasts and feel its rolling gait and to view the
ancient pyramids from that vantage point. But one of the
members of our group got a longer ride than she had bar-
gained for.

As the Young Ambassador returned from her camel ride,
the Egyptian tour guide demanded another dollar before
he would permit her to dismount from his camel. When
she refused, he said something like, "Okay. We take you
around the pyramids again!" My wife, Heidi, and I roared
with laughter as we watched her bounce off again toward
the pyramids on the back of the camel. When the camel
jockey finally brought her back, she promptly paid the
extra dollar and was allowed to dismount.

After exploring the pyramids and the surrounding
areas, we boarded the bus again and traveled to the nearby
papyrus shop. As we exited the bus, we were again surrounded by a swarm of Egyptian salesmen who pressed us
to buy typical tourist items. However, these new salesmen
we encountered were all young boys from about six to
twelve years of age. Most of us ignored their excited pleas
and pushed past them into the shop to learn how papyrus
is made.

After taking this short tour, Heidi and I stepped out of
the shop back into the blistering heat. Our greatest desire
was to get out of the heat and onto the air-conditioned bus,
where we had a stash of bottled water. Before we could
board the bus, though, the group of boys surrounded us

and tried to engage us in conversation. I was trying to be polite, while at the same time trying to brush them off, when one little curly-headed Egyptian boy said in broken English, "Hey! Are you American?" I wanted to escape the heat, but something inside me said, "This is why you came. Now take some time for these young people."

I responded, "Yes, I'm American. How are you guys doing?" He and his friends gathered around and within minutes we began to develop a relationship. When we explained that we were entertainers from America, the curly-headed Egyptian boy perked up and said, "Hey! Do you know Michael Jackson?" When we replied that we did, they got even more excited. They took it to mean that we were personally acquainted with Michael Jackson! From that point on they became our little groupies (because we knew Michael Jackson personally!) and practically worshipped the ground we walked on. It was great—for a few moments, anyway!

In the short time that we visited together, our newfound curly-headed friend just melted our hearts. He and his companions had very little clothing on, and it was obvious that they were very poor. We gave them pens, some Young Ambassador postcards, buttons, and anything else we could find on us. We told them our names, pointed out our pictures on the postcards, and wished that we had more things we could give them. They responded enthusiastically.

We gave one young Egyptian girl a ball point pen, and she immediately used it to write all over her little brother's bare chest. The pen tickled his skin and made him laugh, and she enjoyed the design she was creating, so both were happy.

When the time came for us to leave our young Egyptian friends, Heidi and I stepped onto the bus and moved to our assigned seats, but then opened our window so we could continue to talk to them as they stood outside in the heat. In our brief encounter with these children, Heidi and I had fallen in love with them. We hated to leave. It was apparent that our curly-headed Egyptian friend felt the same way, and he began to search through his little satchel of wares for something he could give to his newfound American friends.

After rummaging through his bag, he pulled out one of his own postcards, held it up to me, and said, "Victor Harris, this postcard for you!" It was a simple gesture, but I'll never forget the feeling of love I experienced. Looking into those beautiful brown eyes, I shared a moment with our little friend that I will always treasure. His eyes were full of love—pure and undefiled—as he stood there holding out his gift to us. I grasped his favorite postcard, thanked him, and said good-bye as the bus began to pull away. Heidi and I spent the next ten minutes in tears as we reflected on the manifestation of love we had just received. There are some moments in life that simply can't be adequately described with words.

I still have that postcard, and I occasionally think about it and what it represents. To me, it represents what the Savior meant when he said we are to "love one another; as I have loved you . . . By this shall all men know that ye are my disciples, if ye have love one to another" (John 13:34–35). I believe that we demonstrate the degree to which the love, the light, and the teachings of Jesus Christ fill our hearts and lives by the way we treat ourselves and treat others.

Do we build up our brothers and sisters, moms and dads, and friends and others with kind words, smiles, hugs, little notes, and other kind acts of service? Or do we tear them down through angry words, hurtful behavior, and neglect? When I ask the question, "What would the Savior do?" I also try to ask, "Will this choice, these words, this action, build up or tear down both me and others?" For me, becoming a moral person, a Saint and not just a

Mormon, a true disciple and not just a follower of Christ, is to learn to make choices that not only build me but that also build others. Only if it builds both me and others is it a moral choice. That is why cutting down, judging, ignoring, and being rude to others is immoral.

Sometimes, making a moral choice can be very difficult. Cleansing the temple in front of his peers was not an easy thing for the Savior to do, but to show respect for his Father and his Father's house was the morally correct decision.

A close friend of mine once visited a rival high school. She was there to participate in an athletic contest as a cheerleader. As she and her friends got off the bus, they were greeted by a crowd of taunting students who abused them with profanity. Offended by the inappropriate use of the Savior's name, my friend demanded that they cease such language. This provoked one young man to taunt her even more with his profane language until, finally, she could take no more of it. She instinctively turned around and kicked him as hard as she could! When she demanded again that he cease such language, he yelled, "What are you, a Mormon or something!" She replied, "Yes I am, and I'm proud of it, too!" Others cheered her courage and began jeering the young man with the foul mouth. He eventually begged her pardon and finally admitted that he was a Mormon too. She then replied, "Well, then, why don't you act like it!" I'm not suggesting that we kick everyone who uses profanity, but there are many times when we must stand tall and make moral choices that are not easy to make.

If a family member or friend is in trouble, or if you know people who are doing self-destructive or immoral things, the difficult moral choice is to inform someone who can help them. Parents, friends, priesthood leaders, or others who are in a position to help need to be advised. Stepping forward in these kinds of circumstances is not easy to do. You may feel you are being disloyal to your wayward friend, but, like the Savior, sometimes we must make the difficult choices we know are right.

May the Lord bless you in the choices you must make. The late Dee Winterton, my Young Ambassador director whom I loved and admired, taught me that service is seldom convenient, but it is always worth it. So it is with moral choices, choices that build and don't tear down others.

I testify to you that this gospel is true and that God lives! I love the spiritual hugs that come from our loving Heavenly Father and Savior when we lift, build, and serve others. In a coming day, I believe we will all look into the eyes of the Savior of the world as we offer him the gifts that we have prepared for him. It is my hope that we will be able to look up at him in love—pure and undefiled—as that little curly-headed Egyptian boy did with me. In that day I hope to say to Him, "I gave and give thee my life. I gave and give thee my love. I give thee the works I have done for others. I give thee all that I am and all that I have become. And I acknowledge from the depths of my soul that thou hast literally made of me a miracle."

In comparison to the marvelous and magnificent things Christ has done for us, our offering may amount only to the worth of a tiny postcard. But it is my prayer that when that long-awaited day comes and we have the glorious opportunity to look into his love-filled eyes and lay before Him the gifts of our lives, that we too, in love—pure and undefiled—will be able to say, "This postcard is for you!"

Victor W. Harris teaches seminary in Logan, Utah. He holds a bachelor's degree in psychology from BYU and is working toward a master's degree in marriage and family relations. He enjoys tennis, basketball, and wrestling, and has performed with BYU's Young Ambassadors and with U.S.O. groups. Victor and his wife, Heidi, have three children.

12

THE GREATEST HERO

Barbara Barrington Jones

All our lives we have had heroes. When we were children, they may have been Batman, Superman, or Wonder Woman. But these superheroes are fantasy characters, always saying and doing the right things and bringing about a happy ending.

That's not real life, is it?

I remember my first hero in high school: Jerri, a gorgeous blonde in my chemistry class. To understand why this girl was my hero, you need to know how I saw myself in the mirror in those days. I was one of the two tallest girls in my class. The other was my best friend, Lynne. I wore my hair slicked back in a ponytail, and I knew my ears stuck out just like Dumbo's. I had a figure like a sausage—absolutely no waistline. And I had feet like canoes, size 10AAA.

Jerri was beautiful. She would stand by her table before chemistry class surrounded by guys who all wanted to talk with her. She was the perfect height. She had long, platinum blonde hair, and a waist as big around as a pencil. We were sure she never had a weekend without a date in her life. I wished I could be just like her. She was my hero.

After high school graduation, I went to New York City

94

to pursue a career as a ballerina. I got a letter from my friend Lynne. She wrote, "Remember Jerri, the gorgeous blonde in our chemistry class? How could we ever forget her? All the boys loved her. She was the center of attention: petite and skinny. She had it all, or so it seemed to us. Well, she tried to commit suicide. She was unsuccessful but is now in a hospital. When I found out, I decided to send her a book, a tape, and some cookies that I had baked, along with a letter telling her how much we had always looked up to her. I was told by her father that she really enjoyed receiving the box and that no one else had cared enough about her to even send a card. He also told me that she had been unhappy and lonely all through high school because she never had any real friends."

When I received that letter in New York, I thought, *Here we assumed she had everything, while in reality she was lonely and so miserable that she had tried to take her own life.* My hero wasn't quite what I had thought.

I had been accepted as a student in the professional class of the New York City Ballet Company. It's not easy to become a classical ballet dancer. There's a ton of competition. The prima ballerina of the company became my hero. She could dance so beautifully. She floated through the classes. She was beautiful, a breathtaking dancer, and thin. I wanted to be just like her.

I thought that in order to be like her, I had to be skinny. I quit eating. I thought it was neat that I could go three whole days without eating anything. I got thinner and thinner and sicker and sicker. I would almost pass out in class. But no matter how much weight I lost, when I looked in the mirror, I saw a fat person. I became so sick and so anemic that I needed to be hospitalized and was sent home. It seemed the dream of my life was over.

Not long after that, the ballerina who was my hero wrote a book called *Dancing on My Grave*. In the book she confessed that she was anorexic and bulimic. She also said that she was addicted to drugs and had taken cocaine and amphetamines to get through all the pain she had inflicted on her body. She had been my hero.

At that point I began attending the University of Arizona. My roommate there was beautiful, with red hair, a perfect figure, and the most gorgeous legs I have ever seen. Again I said to myself, "She's my hero. She's everything I could hope to be."

In those days, it was cool for a girl to smoke. I was not a member of the Church then, and I decided to try it. I remember my first cigarette. I got the worst migraine headache I have ever had. That was my first cigarette and my last. It wasn't too long before I found out some more about my roommate. She had very loose morals and was having an affair with her English professor. And what she was smoking all that time was marijuana. What had happened to my hero?

I went back to El Paso. The boy I had dated all through high school was there. I thought Jimmy was everything I had ever wanted in a man. Even today, speaking his name strikes a chord in my heart. We became engaged and sent out the invitations. I had my bridal gown. The bridesmaids were chosen. Everything was ready. Then one night, Jimmy went to a local bar where he became drunk and violent. He began smashing the windshields of cars with a baseball bat, and he was taken to jail. I discovered he was an alcoholic. The wedding was canceled. My hero had been shown to have feet of clay.

So I married his best friend, John. I didn't love him, but he was a really nice guy. I married him because I thought I was ready to get married. Now I had a new hero. But there was one thing I did not know about John. He was manic-depressive. As a new bride of nineteen, I found my husband lying on the floor of the bathroom, passed out from the effects of swallowing the contents of a whole bottle of aspirin. I had to drag him to the car by myself and rush him to the hospital, where he had his stomach pumped. Not too long after that, he took all my scrapbooks and journals, everything from my school days, into the backyard and burned them.

The worst was yet to come. Three times during the twelve years I was married to him, he pointed a loaded gun at my head. In those moments, I said, "Heavenly Father, are you there?" And each time I felt the comfort of the Spirit. I didn't know what that feeling was, but I knew that God cared about me. Finally, after years of terror, I left. He eventually committed suicide.

Then I met a person worthy to be my hero: my husband, Hal. When we met, I said, "You're my hero."

Hal said, "No, I'm not. I'm just a regular old human being with feet of clay. I think you'd better get right with God." I listened to him. I had been raised in the Catholic church, and I began going to mass every single day. Hal and I got married, and we moved to San Francisco.

There I met a nun and asked her to teach me about the Bible. The first day in the convent, she opened the Bible to Jeremiah 1:5 where it says, "Before I formed thee in the belly I knew thee." I thought to myself, *You did?* This was my Heavenly Father, and I wanted to know him.

My teacher taught me about Jesus Christ, who had said, "I am the way, the truth, and the life: no man cometh unto the Father, but by me" (John 14:6). At that time, I began saying a prayer that would not be answered for five years. Every single night I prayed, "Jesus Christ, who are you? Where are you?"

Then, in the summer of 1979, my husband and I ended up in Salt Lake City during a vacation. We walked into the visitors center on Temple Square where we watched an impressive film. The very last picture on the screen was a picture I had never seen before of the Savior. He was wearing white robes, surrounded by angels, and wearing a red sash around his waist. There in the darkness, he said to me, "Barbara, here I am. Come follow me."

I knew at that moment that he was my true hero, a hero who was able to say, "I am with you alway[s], even unto the end of the world" (Matthew 28:20). A hero who never changes. The one hero in all the world without feet of clay. Christ is always there for us, always ready to forgive, always ready to lift us, always there. All we have to do is come unto Him.

In our lives we do need people to look up to. As my husband used to say, "There's 80 percent of me that's good, and 20 percent that's not so good." We need to pick out the admirable characteristics in people and emulate them, but the great and perfect example in all things is the Savior. If we emulate him, we can never go wrong.

He is the world's greatest hero.

Barbara Barrington Jones is an international image consultant, author, lecturer, and fashion designer. She is a member of the President's Roundtable Advisory Board for BYU-Hawaii, where she also serves on the Education Week planning committee and directs a summer program for women. Barbara and her husband, Hal, have two children.

13

PUTTING ON THE WHOLE ARMOR OF GOD

---◦•◦---

Kory Kunz

It is a commonly known fact that I am the wimpiest semi-nary teacher in the Church. I graduated from high school weighing ninety-eight pounds. My arms were the size of toothpicks—little more than flesh draped around bones. Though I'm a little bigger now, I still need help in a fight. I have learned that if I put on the whole armor of God every day, I can withstand Satan.

Satan is an experienced warrior. He is his own boss, and he has billions of "employees" who work for him. They have had thousands of years of experience battling against your ancestors. They have fought against your great-grandparents, your grandparents, and your parents, and now they fight you. Satan and his employees are very good at their jobs and they are well prepared for you. The Prophet Joseph Smith and Sidney Rigdon saw Satan in a vision, in which they learned that Satan "maketh war with the saints of God, and encompasseth them round about" (D&C 76:29). Who is he fighting against? Drug dealers? Gang members? No! He is fighting against the saints of God—that means you and me.

Who is winning the war, you or Satan? Satan thinks that he is winning. Enoch also saw Satan in a vision and tells us that "[Satan] had a great chain in his hand, and it veiled the whole face of the earth with darkness; and he looked up and laughed, and his angels rejoiced" (Moses 7:26). What a frightening vision! Imagine Satan looking up at Heavenly Father and laughing at him while his angels or employees rejoice over the evil they are spreading.

Satan may think he is winning the war against us, but I know of two evidences that he is not. The first evidence is found in his own name. In the premortal existence he was known as Lucifer, which means "the shining one." Now he is known as Perdition, which means "loss," or, shall we say, "Loser." There is in his very name an indication that he will lose the battle against us and our Heavenly Father.

The second evidence is found in a conversation that took place between Heavenly Father and Satan just after Adam and Eve had partaken of the forbidden fruit. Heavenly Father said to Satan: "I will put enmity between thee and the woman, between thy seed and her seed; and he shall bruise thy head, and thou shalt bruise his heel" (Moses 4:21). In this verse we are told that Eve and all her children (that means us) will be given power to bruise Satan's head, whereas he is given power only to bruise our heel. I've bruised my heel before and it hurts. But it's not likely that you would die from a bruised heel. You'll probably never hear a doctor say, "He died of a bruised heel, the worst bruises I've ever seen. Bruises were all over the heel." But it is quite likely that you could die of a bruised head. So the next time Satan tries to bruise your heel by tempting you to sin, just remember his name—LOSER—and that you have the ability to figuratively crush his head.

When a soldier dresses himself for war, he puts armor on his body to cover his vital body parts. That way, even if the enemy strikes him with his weapons, the soldier is protected from injury or death. Even though Satan is a loser and we have ultimate power over him, we must protect ourselves from his fiery darts. The way we do this is by putting on the whole armor of God. "Put on the whole armour of God, that ye may be able to stand against the wiles of the devil. . . . Stand therefore, having your loins girt about with truth, and having on the breastplate of righteousness; and your feet shod with the preparation of the gospel of peace; above all, taking the shield of faith, wherewith ye shall be able to quench all the fiery darts of the wicked. And take the helmet of salvation, and the sword of the Spirit, which is the word of God" (Ephesians 6:11, 14–17). As sons and daughters of God we can protect ourselves by putting on the whole armor of God.

THE BREASTPLATE OF RIGHTEOUSNESS AND FEET SHOD WITH PEACE

The breastplate covers the vital body parts such as the lungs, heart, liver, and stomach. One of Satan's favorite tactics in the latter days is to attack us in our vitals by tempting us to break the Word of Wisdom.

My brother and I had a unique relationship growing up. I would follow him around and he would hurt me. He would usually slug me on my left shoulder. I had a permanent lump on my left shoulder from his punches. I once asked my mother if she thought it was cancer, and she assured me that it was not.

As a freshman in high school I was an even five feet tall and weighed only eighty-two pounds. My brother, who was only a year older than me in school, was almost six feet tall and weighed 170 pounds. We were opposites. Our family had just moved to Idaho that year to take over my grandpa's farm. We moved from Kansas and were building a house. One day, while the builders were laying brick, my brother and I were walking around the house and he said, "I wonder what mortar tastes like." I told him I had no idea and continued walking. Then he said, "Kory, I want you to eat some mortar and tell me what it tastes like." I told him, "No way," and he said, "Do it or suffer the consequences." He had used that line on me many times before and I had always given in, afraid of what the consequences might be. For fear of being slugged in my cancerous arm, I took a handful of mortar, put it in my mouth, chewed, and swallowed. It was gritty, thick, and got kind of hard as it went down. I get the shivers just thinking about it today. But at least I didn't have to "suffer the consequences."

I remember hating Sunday nights because my brother and I had the responsibility of milking the cows, so my dad could have the evening off. There were many instruments of torture in the barn. My brother's favorite torture device was a black hose. The black hoses hung down next to the three cow milking stalls and were used to clean the cows' udders and get them ready for milking. They were high-pressure hoses that carried freezing cold water. My brother would often demand, "Spray yourself in the face for five seconds with that hose." I would tell him, "No way." And he would warn me, "Do it or suffer the consequences." I would think about the possible consequences and commence spraying. I remember the stinging and numbing sensation and how my eyelids would flap up and down painfully under the force of the water.

One day my brother and I were out in the cow pasture, and he said to me, "I wonder what cow manure tastes like." I don't remember him saying, "Do it or suffer the consequences," but I do remember thinking about my cancerous arm and then deciding to eat the cow manure. Now, I'm really not a connoisseur of cow manure, but I found a specimen that was probably about two weeks old. I can only say that it was better than the mortar. It tasted kind of like grass and dirt mixed together.

A year went by and I did some changing—physically. I became a sophomore. I didn't weigh eighty-two pounds anymore, I weighed eighty-seven, and I grew to a height of five feet, one inch. My brother did some changing that summer also. He decided that drinking and chewing tobacco were going to be a part of his life. I knew all about his new habits but chose to tell no one for fear of my life.

One day my brother and I were going into town to go to a stake dance. Our second cousin, who was also my brother's best friend, was riding shotgun, and I was sitting between them in the pickup truck. They were both chewing tobacco. All of a sudden my brother reached into his pocket, pulled out a little white pouch of tobacco, and handed it to me. "Here," he said, "put this under your lip; it's chewing tobacco." Now there was a moment of truth! At my brother's insistence, I had eaten mortar, sprayed myself in the face, eaten cow manure, and done a hundred other things that I don't have time to tell you about, and now I was being told to chew tobacco. Not just by anyone, but by my big brother—my big brother whom I both feared and loved dearly. I held the tobacco in my hand, looked at it, gave it back to him, and asked him to drop me off at the dance. I braced myself for a "Do it or suffer the consequences," or a punch to my cancerous arm, but nothing came. Instead, he turned the pickup around and took me to the dance. Though I was undoubtedly the wimpiest boy at that dance, I felt strong and powerful because I had recognized Satan and his tactics and had succeeded in crushing his head.

My brother continued his way of life for a year or so and then recognized his mistakes. He decided to put on the whole armor of God and to get his feet "shod" in preparation to spread the gospel. Peace came into his life as he repented of his sins and grew closer to Christ. He served an incredibly successful mission and has been a shining example to me ever since. I dearly love my brother. Being a member missionary and serving a full-time mission are excellent ways to keep Satan from penetrating your body and spirit with his fiery darts.

THE HELMET OF SALVATION
AND THE SHIELD OF FAITH

The helmet protects your head, the place that houses your mind and your thoughts. Regarding pornographic materials, President Ezra Taft Benson counseled, "[Do] not pollute your minds with such degrading matter, for the mind through which this filth passes is never the same afterwards. Don't see R-rated movies or vulgar videos or participate in any entertainment that is immoral, suggestive, or pornographic. Don't listen to music that is degrading" (*Ensign*, May 1986, p. 45).

My wife comes from a family of thirteen children. Her brother Brian was twelve years old in 1982. He was invited to his first video party and was very excited when he arrived at his friend's house. Surrounded by all of his friends, he sat down to watch the video. Ten minutes into the video he saw something he had never seen before. He saw an immoral scene. He had not been told the name of the movie and did not know that it was R-rated. He had never seen an R-rated movie before. Making a quick decision, he stood up, walked into the kitchen, and stood there for the next two hours while his friends finished watching the video. He felt so badly for having watched the part he had seen that he spent a lot of time on his knees that night asking for forgiveness. The following Sunday, he sat down next to his father and tapped him on his shoulder. "I've sinned, Dad," he said, with tears in his eyes.

"What did you do?" his father asked.

"I watched about ten minutes of an R-rated video and saw something really terrible. Do you think I should go see the bishop?" Brian knew how serious it was to pollute his mind with Satan's filthiness. He promised his dad that he would never see another video like that again. His chance came a couple of weeks later. There was another video party with his friends. This time he asked them in advance the name of the video. After they told him, he said, "Isn't that an R-rated video?" "Yes, but it's not a bad R," they replied. Again Brian went to the kitchen, this time not to stand, but to call for a ride home.

Three months later, on December 28, 1982, Brian was killed in a snowmobiling accident. He left this life not being perfect, but knowing that he had done his best to keep Satan from polluting his mind with filthy and degrading matter. Brian used *the shield of faith* to protect him. Faith shielded him from the polluting videos his friends watched. He had discovered a great truth—that it is not physical death that we should fear, but spiritual death.

GIRD YOUR LOINS WITH TRUTH AND WIELD THE SWORD OF THE SPIRIT

Immorality is one of Satan's favorite weapons today. Perhaps the only way to stay morally clean is to wield *the sword of the Spirit*. It is the one offensive weapon that comes with God's armor. I believe that we need to go on the offensive against Satan when he tries to tempt us to be immoral.

Elder L. Tom Perry tells the story of a beautiful girl who was the only member of the Church in her class in school. Everyone knew that she expected all of her dates to live by her standards if they wanted to go out with her. One day the school football hero came up to her before the most special dance of the year and said, "You know, I would ask you to go to the dance with me if you would lower your standards just a little." There was no hesitation in her voice when she replied, "If I would go out with you, I would be lowering my standards" (*Ensign*, November 1979, p. 36). She wasn't about to let the desire to go to a school dance or the chance to date a popular guy dictate her standards.

There is one final tactic to use against Satan. It is found in D&C 38:42: "And go ye out from among the wicked.

Save yourselves. Be ye clean that bear the vessels of the Lord." Sometimes, the best thing to do is run away from evil. I promise that if you will put on the whole armor of God and go out from among the wicked, you truly will save yourself. You *will* be clean and you *will* conquer Satan.

Kory Kunz teaches seminary in Vernal, Utah. He holds a bachelor's degree in communications from the University of Utah and served a Spanish-speaking mission in Tampa, Florida. Kory is a singer and songwriter and currently serves as ward mission leader.

14

TRUE GREATNESS

Steven T. Linford

I'm an avid sports fan! I look forward to enjoying fall afternoons and the cool air and the changing leaves as I leave my home to attend a football game. I love the excitement of the game: last-second comebacks, underdogs achieving victory, anticipation, bone-crushing tackles, and the overall energy of the game. In the winter I love to be in a packed gym, loaded with fans supporting their teams, a good band, cheering, good defense, incredible shooting, dunking, yelling! Wow! Just thinking about it makes the hair rise on my arms. High school, college, or professional sports, it doesn't matter. Just let me watch a ball game (with some chips), and I'm happy.

The fun of participating in and watching sports is diminished for me by one aspect of the game that turns my stomach. It happens only sometimes, usually at the end of a game or a match. It happens when an athlete who is being honored for his or her play begins to boast. Comments such as, "I'm the greatest"; "I'm the greatest in the world"; "I'm the greatest in the universe"; "I'm the champion"; "I'm the best"; "No one is even close to my greatness" . . . Oh, yuck! I think I'm going to be sick. On the other hand, I love to see a truly great but modest athlete receive post-game honors. You know the type. He or she stands humbly, usually covered with sweat, always gracious, slow to accept any personal credit, quick to praise his or her coach and teammates and to acknowledge the efforts of the opposing team. This athlete seems uncomfortable to be honored and would rather be in the locker room celebrating with teammates.

Let me tell you about one of the greatest athletes I have ever met. This athlete, Todd, wasn't large or rippling with muscles or bursting with talent. In fact, he was quite lanky and skinny. He wasn't the star; in fact, he wasn't a very good player at all. But, in my mind, he stood above the rest. He didn't play school ball. He tried, but he was cut. Todd played church ball, and he provided me one of the most important lessons concerning sports and life that I have ever been taught. Todd was in my ninth-grade seminary class; I was his part-time seminary teacher.

I quickly grew to love Todd. He had an air of purity, of innocence about him. One day Todd burst into my classroom and exclaimed, "Brother Linford, I played church ball last night, and it was so fun!" I immediately began wondering about his stats. I said, "That's great, Todd! How many points did you have?" Todd responded, "I didn't score any points." I replied, "Oh, sometimes that happens, and it's okay. I bet you had a lot of assists and rebounds." His eyes still filled with excitement, Todd said, "I didn't get a rebound or an assist. In fact," he continued, "I didn't even get to play in the game. But I had a great time warming up with my team before the game, and shooting during half-time." There was a pause and then I realized that I was standing in front of one of the greatest athletes, one of the greatest people, I had ever met. While I was evaluating greatness from a worldly perspective (stats), he was teaching me a higher or better measuring device, one based on selflessness and humility.

We are living in a world where greatness is usually

defined by things such as money, popularity, where we live, what we wear, and what we drive. But I know that our Heavenly Father measures greatness in another way. What we read in 1 Samuel 16:7 is true: "Man [looks] on the outward appearance" (including fame and fortune), "but the Lord [looks] on the heart."

President Ezra Taft Benson defined true greatness this way: "That man [or young man or young woman] is greatest and most blessed and joyful whose life most closely approaches the pattern of the Christ. This has nothing to do with earthly wealth, power, or prestige. The only true test of greatness, blessedness, joyfulness is how close a life can come to being like the Master, Jesus Christ. He is the right way, the full truth, and the abundant life" (*Ensign*, December 1988, p. 2).

True greatness has little to do with the number of letters on our letterman jacket, the number of musical instruments we play, or the number of clubs or organizations to which we belong. True greatness has to do with becoming like Jesus Christ and treating people as Jesus treated them.

Over the years of teaching the gospel in seminary and at BYU, I have seen countless Christlike acts performed by many impressive youth. One outstanding young woman who had a marvelous ability to make people feel special was Alexis. I recall seeing Alexis for the first time one fall evening at a football game on a Friday before school was to start. Being new to the area, I did not know anyone. I went to the game by myself, hoping to hear some names or see some faces that I would recognize in my seminary class the next Monday.

The game was exciting and the crowd was into it, alternately cheering and groaning. Sitting by myself, wearing a big "L" (for loner) on my forehead, I overheard a conversation between two elderly women. One lady turned to the other and asked, "Do you see that young woman down there?" The other woman inquired which young woman she was talking about. Her friend replied, "The one on the end. Her name is Alexis." I looked down to where the lady was pointing, and took note of the girl whose name was Alexis. She was one of the cheerleaders.

On the first day of school, as the students began pouring into the seminary building, I saw Alexis come in. Wearing a big smile on her lovely face, she immediately extended her hand and said, "Hi, what's your name?" We shook hands and I responded, "I'm Brother Linford, a new seminary teacher, and I already know who you are. You are Alexis." Something clicked between us and we instantly became friends. Each day when she came to seminary, she would find me and would usually say, "Hi, Brother L." I didn't teach her that year, her junior year, but her teacher said she was an absolute joy in the classroom.

A year passed, and I found that I would be teaching Alexis her senior year. I quickly discovered what her previous teacher meant. Alexis was an impressive young woman. She had won a beauty pageant, had been a cheerleader, and was on the drill team. She was involved in drama, she was a member of the seminary council, and she worked as a lifeguard at the local swimming pool. She had every opportunity to be self-centered and stuck-up. But she was anything but that way. Instead, she loved everyone, she treated everyone kindly, and everyone was her friend.

One day Alexis was in charge of presenting the devotional we held at the beginning of each class. What she did was amazing. She gave a short talk in which she described the unconditional love that Heavenly Father has for all his children. She also said that we all have talents and that it doesn't matter which talents we have as long as we use them. Then she explained that she wanted to do something different as a part of her devotional. She turned to a young man named Greg, and mentioned several things she admired about him. Then she had Greg turn and tell the person sitting behind him some of the reasons he admired her. Each student took a turn, first listening to positive comments about himself or herself, and in turn expressing admiration of the positive qualities of another classmate. By the end of the devotional there was a powerful feeling of love in the classroom. This is just one example of the unique ability Alexis had to make people feel special and important. Throughout the entire school year, she brought that kind of spirit to class.

One day, about a month before school ended, Alexis rushed into class with some friends. She asked if it would be okay if we took some class time to bear testimonies. I took her suggestion, and following our devotional we had a testimony meeting. Alexis was one who stood that day. I remember her testimony well. It was the last public testimony that I recall her giving. In it, she expressed her love for everyone in the class, for her family, and for the Savior. She said that He was her best friend. She challenged us to love and accept ourselves for who we are: children of our Heavenly Father. After hearing her, I again felt uplifted by her example and testimony.

One of the last times I saw Alexis was during the last week of school. She was sitting on the steps of the seminary building after school one day with a young man who had been having some difficulty in his life. The next morning I saw Alexis at an early morning fireside, and I asked her if she had been able to help him. She replied that he was going to be okay.

A few weeks after school ended, I received word that there had been a terrible accident that had claimed the lives of two young people. A few days later I found myself speaking at "Lex's" funeral. In spite of the awful loss we all experienced because of Alexis's untimely death, I felt comforted knowing that she had lived a life that was pleasing to her Heavenly Father. Her life had "closely approach[ed] the pattern of the Christ," and she had succeeded in following the Savior's advice when he declared,

"What manner of men [and women] ought ye to be? Verily I say unto you, even as I am" (3 Nephi 27:27).

On June 6, 1994, our newly ordained prophet, President Howard W. Hunter, made this statement at a press conference: "I would invite all members of the Church to live with ever-more attention to the life and example of the Lord Jesus Christ, especially the love and hope and compassion He displayed. I pray that we might treat each other with more kindness, more courtesy, more humility and patience and forgiveness."

I once heard about a young man I'll call Phil, who certainly exemplified these wonderful qualities. This young man played baseball on the school team, and would later play college baseball. During his senior year in high school, he was asked by his seminary teacher if he would sit next to and befriend a particular young woman in his seminary class. Amy had mental and physical disabilities and struggled to do even the most basic tasks. Phil's teacher asked him if he would sit by Amy and help her in any way that he could. The young man accepted the opportunity. Throughout the year Phil helped this special friend. Together they would find and mark things in her scriptures and work on her assignments and on tests. He became good friends with her. As the year went on, the time for the girls-choice dance approached. One night Phil received a very creative invitation to go to the dance. He assumed that he was being asked by a young woman he had been dating. But, much to his surprise, he found that he was being asked by Amy, the girl who sat next to him in his seminary class. Then, to complicate matters, he was asked to go to the dance by the girl he had been dating. He had a difficult decision to make. Should he go with Amy, or should he go with the girl he had been dating? He talked to his "girlfriend" about his dilemma. She insisted that he go with her and not with his seminary friend. After all, she argued, everyone knew they were "going together."

Well, the young man finally made his difficult decision. He would go with Amy, who had asked him first.

Finally, the night of the dance came. The couple went to dinner, then to the dance, and had their picture taken together. It was a night to remember. Later, Amy's mother thanked Phil for his kindness and thoughtfulness by saying, "You are the only true friend my daughter has ever had."

President Gordon B. Hinckley has reminded us: "This is a season to be strong. . . . It is a time to be found keeping the commandments. It is a season to reach out with kindness and love to those in distress and to those who are wandering in darkness and pain. It is a time to be considerate and good, decent and courteous toward one another in all of our relationships. In other words, to become more Christlike" (*Ensign,* May 1995, p. 71).

I remember one story that a proud father told at his son's missionary farewell. It was about his missionary son, Brian, who at the time the story took place had been a junior in high school. Brian was a starter on the high school soccer team, a team that had been playing well and had secured a berth in the state championship soccer tournament. Brian's team had been winning games and had advanced to the semifinals. The winner of that game would continue to the state championship game; the loser would go home. The semifinal game began, and both teams played well. At the end of regulation play the score was tied. There would need to be a shoot-off. During the shoot-off a player from each team would have a chance for a free kick, an opportunity to score a goal. If both players missed, others on the teams would each take a turn until one team scored and the other missed in the same round. The shoot-off began and the opposing team went first. Their player kicked the ball, and it was successfully blocked by the goalie. A player from Brian's team then took his turn at a free kick, and he too did not score. Other players took their turns, one after another, alternating back and forth between teams. Finally, a player from the opposing team managed to score a goal. Under the pressure and excitement that is automatically built into state play-off games, a player from Brian's team approached to kick the ball. If he scored the goal, the game would be tied and the shoot-off would continue. If he missed, the game would be over, and the opposing team would advance to the state championship game. The player approached the ball and kicked, the ball sailed through the air, the opposing goalie reacted and with outstretched arms was able to bat the ball away from the goal. The opposing team had won and immediately began celebrating on the field. The losing players hung their heads and began leaving the field. The dejected player who had missed the goal lay motionless, face down on the grass. The fans began exiting the stands, walking around and avoiding the player who had just missed scoring the goal. Brian's father recounted the scene as he had viewed it from the stands: the fans and defeated players leaving, the victorious team celebrating, the dejected player lying on the ground. Then the father saw something that deeply impressed him. He saw his son jog across the field toward the dejected player. Brian reached the player, bent over, whispered something into his ear, and then helped his teammate up from the ground. Brian put his arm around his buddy, and the two young men left the field together. The father commented at the farewell that his son's simple act of compassion, performed after the season was over, meant more to him than the play of his son on the soccer field all season long.

Each of us occasionally comes into contact with a person who figuratively has his or her face in the grass, who feels dejected, who feels like a loser. If we are to follow the example of our Savior, we need to reach out, whisper encouraging words, put our arm around such people, and help them get beyond the difficult and disappointing times. In President Hinckley's words, we need "to reach out with kindness and love to those in distress and to those who are wandering in darkness and pain."

The scriptures contain many beautiful accounts of how the Savior lifted and built people up. One such account is of the Savior passing through Jericho, a city where a man named Zacchaeus was living. Zacchaeus was a rich tax collector. As you can well imagine, tax collectors weren't especially popular at the time of Christ, especially rich tax collectors. As the people gathered to see Jesus, Zacchaeus, who was "little of stature," was crowded out. He tried, but could not see because he was short and possibly because of the unwillingness of the people to let a despised publican stand with them. So what did Zacchaeus do? He climbed a tree so that he could catch a glimpse of Jesus. As the Savior reached the place where Zacchaeus was, he looked up at him, and, knowing the needs of Zacchaeus, said to him, "Make haste, and come down; for to day I must abide at thy house." The next verse states, "And he made haste, and came down, and received him joyfully" (Luke 19:1–6). The Savior extended kindness and love to an individual who was probably not very popular, to an individual who it appears was not allowed to be part of the crowd. We need to take similar care to serve those who are somehow placed in our path.

Another example of Jesus treating people with compassion is the account of his encounter with the woman accused of adultery. Early one morning Jesus went to the temple in Jerusalem. While teaching the people there, Jesus was presented a woman who her accusers said had been caught in the act of adultery. Wishing perhaps to embarrass Jesus, these men asked what should be done to this woman. The law of Moses prescribed stoning for such an offense. Should they proceed, they wanted to know, to stone her to death? Jesus at first ignored the hypocritical accusers, then finally said to them, "He that is without sin

among you, let him first cast a stone at her." One by one
the men left until only Jesus and the woman remained.
Jesus then inquired of the woman, "Woman, where are
those thine accusers? hath no man condemned thee?" The
woman responded, "No man, Lord." And Jesus said to her,
"Neither do I condemn thee: go, and sin no more" (John
8:2–11). Jesus did not forgive her; she would still have to
pass through the process of repentance herself. But he
treated her with respect and minimized her embarrass-
ment. Jesus did not condone the sin, but neither did he
condemn the sinner. He kindly set her on the path of
repentance.

During the last week of his mortal ministry, Jesus taught,
"Inasmuch as ye have done it unto [served] one of the least
of these my brethren, ye have done it unto me" (Matthew
25:40). Who are those Jesus described as the "least of
these"? Don't you suppose they are those who are sick,
those with few friends, those who endure difficult family
situations, those who are feeling distress and pain? How
about those who are lonely, those who are afraid, those
who are wandering in spiritual darkness, and those who
have sinned? In truth, the category of those who need help
includes everyone to some degree, at some point in life. As
we are helping and serving other people, we are actually
helping and serving Jesus Christ.

It is important to remember that we will not become
completely like the Savior overnight, this week, or even
this year. We will not become perfect in this life. But we
must not become discouraged. We need to remind ourselves that it takes time, that the Lord doesn't expect us to
become perfect in all things while we are here on the earth.
He expects us to try our best, to live today a little better
than we lived yesterday. When we have done all we can,
then he will make up the difference, and perfection will be
attainable.

I love the words of a favorite Primary song:

> *I'm trying to be like Jesus;*
> *I'm following in his ways.*
> *I'm trying to love as he did,*
> *In all that I do and say.*
> *At times I am tempted to make a wrong choice,*
> *But I try to listen as the still small voice*
> *Whispers, "Love one another as Jesus loves you.*
> *Try to show kindness in all that you do.*
> *Be gentle and loving in deed and in thought,*
> *For these are the things Jesus taught."*
> *(Janice Kapp Perry,* Children's Songbook, *p. 78)*

I know you are truly great! You exemplify so many of the qualities of Jesus Christ. You are blessing and lifting those around you. I hope that we all will recognize true greatness in others and in ourselves, not measured by worldly accomplishments, but more importantly by how much we follow the example of our Savior, Jesus Christ.

Steven T. Linford graduated from the University of Utah and holds a master's degree from Utah State University. He is currently working toward a Ph.D. at BYU. He has served in a variety of Church callings, including Primary and Scouting and as a bishopric and high council member. He loves to play basketball, run, bike, swim, and spend time with his family.

15

"OF THAT DAY AND HOUR KNOWETH NO MAN"

Allen Litchfield

Dr. Martin Luther King presented his powerful and poignant "I Have a Dream" sermon in Washington, D.C., in 1963. People have been quoting from it ever since. This little article does not pretend to be of that calibre, but "I Have a Nightmare," and I want to tell you about it. The setting of my nightmare is not a haunted house and does not involve a Jason- or Freddy-character trying to kill me. You may have heard that in those horror movies, the bad guy has been brutally murdering people left and right. So the next victim decides to go all alone, with no weapons, in the dark, to the spookiest place around to investigate. Does this make sense to you?

But my nightmare is much scarier than that. My nightmare takes place in a high school or college class. And it is even more horrifying than those nightmares where you arrive in class in your underwear. In my scary dream the professor comes into the room on the first day of class and seems sort of normal—no fangs, no Satanic symbols tattooed on his face, no hockey mask, no chain saw. But here is the scary part: the teacher says that the date of the final exam will not be fixed. The final exam will determine entirely whether we pass the class or not, but we won't know when the final will be given until just before it takes place. The final exam might be handed out today or tomorrow, or it might be next week or near the end of the semester. The exam won't necessarily even be given during class time. It could be at midnight on a Friday night, after the big dance, or on Sunday at six in the morning, before the paperboy comes. The exam might be given during the summer holidays or on Christmas Day. Even though this sounds ridiculous, the final exam might not even be given in this school year; it could take place years or even decades from now, after some of us have moved away to other towns. The teacher gives all the students "beepers" and tells us that when the beeper goes off, we must come immediately and take the final exam.

In other words, we must always be ready, and we can never relax and forget about the class. We can't wait until the night before to prepare because we will never know on any particular night before, that the test will take place the next day. Being always ready to take the final exam is not something most students are good at or enjoy. In my nightmare, all the students drop the class immediately because they can't handle the stress of being continually prepared for the rest of their lives.

However, in real life, in some ways, we are all in that kind of situation. And we don't have the option of dropping the class or skipping the final because the reason we are here on earth is to prepare for the final exam. We don't know the date of the Judgment Day, or whether we will pass away before the Second Coming of the Lord. There is no way to know when that "great and terrible day" will come. But there is no need to panic. Let me tell you how this seeming nightmare of uncertainty can be turned into an amazing dream.

The Lord Jesus Christ has promised that he will return to the earth to judge the people and rule and reign. This Second Coming is a literal event, not just a point in time that will usher in an era of peace. Our Lord is really going to return to the earth. He has given us some clues about the timing of his second coming, which he called "the signs of the times" (Matthew 16:3). The scriptures contain some things to watch for as the time approaches, but "some have wrested the scriptures, and have gone far astray because of this thing" (Alma 41:1). To "wrest" the scriptures is to "twist or turn" them in a way that was not intended. I believe that when we try to nail down the exact time of the Second Coming from the Lord's word, we are wresting the scriptures, or using them in a way that they were not intended. Let me explain the difference between *accurate* and *precise*, at least in the way that I am using the words, so that you will see what I mean.

Accurate means correct or right, in conformity with truth, without error or defect. The signs of the times regarding Christ's second coming are accurate. *Precise* means exact, specific, detailed, expressed in a definite and absolute way that cannot be misunderstood. The signs of the times are not precise (at least as to "when" the event is to take place). A few examples of the difference might make the whole thing more clear. (1) Since I weigh more than 200 pounds, if I said that I weighed 147.239 pounds, that statement would be precise, but not accurate. If I said I weighed more than 200 pounds, that statement would be accurate, but not very precise. (2) Look at my picture at the end of this article; if I said I was 29 years, 2 months, 27 days, and 11 hours old right now, would that statement be accurate or precise? You are right: although that statement is precise, very exact, it is simply not true or accurate. But if I said I was over 40 years old, that statement would be accurate but not so specific that you would know precisely how old I am. (Looking at my picture you might guess that I was 60, which I am not; but even if I were, the statement about being over 40 would still be accurate.)

Now, if we apply these same principles to the signs of

the times, we can benefit by seeing the truth of the prophecies, without falsely concluding that we can come up with exact timing. (1) If we were to say that Jesus will return to the earth on April 6, 2000, shortly after 3:00 P. M., Jerusalem time, that would be precise, but we have no way of knowing how accurate it is. (2) If I were to claim that the Second Coming would certainly be in my lifetime, that would not be a precise statement, but even that imprecise conclusion could not be confirmed for accuracy. (3) If we were to say that Jesus will come again and that his coming is near at hand, even at the doors, that statement would not be precise, but it would be completely accurate. (4) If we were to declare that the prophets and Church leaders will keep us up to date as to how we must prepare for the Second Coming, that statement would give no precise information about dates, but would be totally accurate.

Throughout Christian history, some people—even a few Latter-day Saints—have combed the scriptures, especially Revelation, Daniel, Ezekiel, and obscure passages from here and there, in an attempt to determine exactly, often to the very day and hour, when Jesus will return. So that we don't waste our time and energy on that futile project, the Lord has told us repeatedly that "the hour and the day no man knoweth, neither the angels in heaven," and once he even added, "nor shall they know until he comes" (D&C 49:7). The Lord wants us to be prepared, however, and says, "Be ye also ready: for in such an hour as ye think not the Son of man cometh" (Matthew 24:44).

Our Lord Jesus Christ will return to the earth in glory. "For the time is at hand; the day or the hour no man knoweth; but it surely shall come" (D&C 39:21). For very good reasons, he has not revealed the exact time of his return. Examining the information given in Matthew 24 and 25 may help us understand how the Lord wants us to occupy ourselves until he returns. Sitting with the Savior on the Mount of Olives, just a few days before he would die for us, the Apostles asked him, "When shall these things be? and what shall be the sign of thy coming, and of the end of the world?" (Matthew 24:3).

In response to their questions, Jesus first presented some signs of the times. He talked about false Christs, false prophets, wars, troubles and afflictions, missionaries going out to all the world, tribulations and desolations, signs in the heavens, and so on. Nothing he said would allow us to figure out exactly when he would be returning, and that seems to have been his design. Instead, the Savior has revealed these signs, so that the believers can be protected somewhat from the worst effects of these events, especially loss of faith and direction. "Behold, I speak these things unto you for the elect's sake; . . . see that ye be not troubled, for all I have told you must come to pass; but the end is not yet" (JS–M 1:23). Knowing the signs of the times allows the Saints to take courage and hold to the plan of God even in times of great difficulty.

After rehearsing the signs, Christ told a parable about a master who goes away, leaving his servant with instructions. The master, who represents the Savior in the story, "shall come in a day when he looketh not for him, and in an hour that he is not aware of" (Matthew 24:50). The idea of the parable seems to be that we, the servants of the Lord, must serve with wisdom and faith, always remaining ready for his return. Our best efforts should be directed toward doing the right things and living the right ways for the right reasons, rather than attempting to calculate the right time.

In the following chapter, Matthew 25, to make that point even clearer, Jesus tells three parables that let us know what we should be about. None of the parables has to do with trying to determine the time of the Second Coming. None of the characters in the parables that represents you or me—the ten virgins, the three servants, or the sheep and goats—is rewarded or punished on the basis of how precisely he or she determined the arrival time of the Lord. Instead, all the parables tell us how we ought to be living, so that we will always be ready whenever he comes.

The first of the three parables is about ten young women who are waiting, lamps in hand, to attend a wedding. The bridegroom whose arrival they are awaiting is the Savior. Five of the young women are wise and prepared, even when the bridegroom tarries or fails to arrive when they expect. Five are foolish young women who want to attend the wedding and who understand the requirements of admission and have their lamps ready—but they fail to maintain their supply of oil. When the call comes at a time that they do not expect, they are forced to scramble to fill their lamps, and they fail to gain entrance to the great wedding. The parable ends with an admonition to "Watch therefore, for ye know neither the day nor the hour wherein the Son of man cometh" (Matthew 25:13). The five wise young women had no better information about the arrival time of the bridegroom than the five foolish—that is not what separated them. The five who succeeded in gaining admission to the feast and who were privileged to "sup" with the bridegroom, our Savior, were the ones living lives of righteousness.

The second parable is about three servants who receive differing amounts of money (a talent is a certain weight of gold) for which they are to be responsible. They are to invest the money and use it wisely till their lord returns. The talents or money represent all that the Lord has given us, probably especially the blessings of the gospel, which he expects us to use for good. The first and second servants risk their gifts and are able to return to their master double the amounts they had been given. Each is told he is a "good and faithful servant" and is invited to "enter thou into the joy of thy lord" (Matthew 25:23). The third servant does not fare so well. It isn't that he doesn't have as clear an idea when the lord will be returning; he simply isn't doing the things he must do and taking advantage of the opportunities that are his. He has hidden or failed to expand on all the gospel blessings that were his, and as a consequence, he loses those blessings and is cast out.

Finally, Jesus tells a parable of the Son of man coming in his glory, sitting in judgment on the nations, and separating the sheep from the goats, the righteous from the unrighteous. The goats don't say anywhere in the parable that they wished they had figured out more precisely when the Lord was coming. The sheep are not heard to say that the reason they were found to be valiant was that they had been able to determine the exact time of the Lord's coming and so were able to arrange to be doing good things just as he arrived. What separated the goats from the sheep was the life each was leading.

The people represented by the sheep were continually—all the time prior to the coming of the Lord—helping the hungry, relieving the thirsty, succoring the stranger, clothing the naked, serving the sick, and comforting the captive. Those kinds of assistance symbolize doing good to people in need, but especially administering the relief of the gospel message to those who need it so much to be spiritually filled, accepted, covered, healed, and freed. The good people who are gathered in with the sheep are told that "Inasmuch as ye have done it unto one of the least of these my brethren, ye have done it unto me" (Matthew 25:40). Without knowing the exact arrival time of their Lord, they have been thoroughly occupied in service and obedience. It wouldn't matter when the Lord arrived, they would have been found ready.

I bear my testimony that Jesus will return in power and glory to the earth. I have very little exact information about when that will be, but that doesn't have to be a nightmare, because I have a great quantity of details about what I ought to be doing now to prepare for his coming. The scriptures and the modern prophets tell me how I should be living. Fear and trepidation about the great and terrible day of the Lord turn into anticipation and delight because "if ye are prepared ye shall not fear" (D&C 38:30). I hope and pray that we will prepare now for his coming. A final piece of great news is that we can allow him to come into our lives and hearts now, prior to his actual coming in glory to the earth. When this happens, the nightmare is dispelled and replaced by a wonderful dream.

Jesus has promised us that he stands at the door, and is asking to be invited into our lives. To all those who hear his voice and open the door, our Savior pledges he will "come in to him, and will sup with him, and he with me" (Revelation 3:20). I testify that we can experience the greatest levels of joy and peace in this life by having the Master sup with us. The Savior calls out to us in modern scripture: forsake your sins, come unto me, call on my name, obey my voice, and keep my commandments, and you "shall see my face and know that I am" (D&C 93:1). Nothing can match the feeling of security and happiness that will result from seeing our Savior's face and knowing that he is. I have a dream that you and I will prepare ourselves and live in such a way that our Lord can come into our lives now.

Allen Litchfield is a religion instructor at Brigham Young University and serves as a high councilor in his Orem, Utah, stake. He served a mission to Tonga and has worked as a seminary teacher and principal and as an institute instructor and director. Allen and his wife, Gladys, have six children.

16

SOME FRIENDLY ADVICE

Max H. Molgard

During the summer months, my family spends a lot of time floating and fishing on the Snake River in Wyoming. A few years ago on a clear but somewhat chilly day, we were at the take-out boat ramp where the float trips end. It was still early in the season, and we felt it was too cold to float, so we were there as spectators checking out the more adventurous souls who were floating the river that chilly day. As we watched the various boats come in, one of them caught our undivided attention. A young man in the boat had apparently fallen in the water on his trip down the river and was soaked from head to toe. His uncontrollable shivering tipped us off immediately that he was in trouble. Those of us with first aid training knew that his body temperature had dropped to dangerous levels and that hypothermia was setting in.

As the boat pulled up to the ramp, a man standing next to us sprinted to his car, grabbed a sleeping bag, and ran back to the ramp. The man helped the boy remove his wet clothes, except for his underwear. He instructed the shivering boy to get into the sleeping bag, and after stripping off his own outside clothing, the man crawled into the sleeping bag with the boy. He wrapped his body around the boy and instructed others to strap the sleeping bag around them, creating a snug cocoon. The moments that followed were tense and critical. We all watched and prayed that the boy's body temperature would respond favorably to the treatment.

Several minutes passed. The boy seemed to relax and his shivering became less severe. As he stabilized, others bundled him into a car and transported him to the nearest hospital to receive further treatment. The quick-thinking man with the sleeping bag had literally saved the boy's life.

We all breathed a sigh of relief as they pulled away. But reflecting on this incident brought a lot of frightening "what ifs" to our minds. What if the boy had been on the river by himself and no one had been at the dock when he arrived? What if the man had left the boy's wet clothes on? And even worse, what if the man's clothes had been wet when he crawled into the bag and wrapped himself around the boy? The answer is obvious: The boy would have died.

Ecclesiastes 4:9–11 states: "Two are better than one; because they have a good reward for their labour. For if they fall, the one will lift up his fellow: but woe to him that is alone when he falleth; for he hath not another to help him up. Again, if two lie together, then they have heat: but how can one be warm alone?"

This passage of scripture points out the value of our having good friends. In fact, there is nothing quite as precious as good friends. On the other hand, there is nothing quite as destructive as bad friends. The question then arises, "How can I know the difference between good and bad friends?" Elder Robert L. Simpson answered that question for us when he taught that real friends "encourage you in 'every thing which inviteth to do good,' as stated by Moroni" (in Conference Report, October 1963, p. 104).

A real friend would never ask us to lower our standards or to do something that might be harmful. Elder Robert D.

Hales described true friendship when he said: "Do you know how to recognize a true friend? A real friend loves us and protects us. In recognizing a true friend we must look for two important elements in that friendship: A true friend makes it easier for us to live the gospel by being around him. Similarly, a true friend does not make us choose between his way and the Lord's way" (*Ensign*, May 1990, p. 40).

The 1955 World Series is one that many people will never forget, partly because of a famous catch by a man named Sandy Amoros.

The memorable game was played on 4 October 1955 at Yankee Stadium. The Brooklyn Dodgers and the New York Yankees had each won three games, forcing a seventh and deciding game for the championship. It was in the sixth inning, with the Dodgers leading 2–0, that Yogi Berra of the New York Yankees came to the plate. Berra hit a fly ball almost to the fence but was ruled out when Sandy Amoros made a running catch that is considered one of the best in World Series history. This catch started a double play that preserved the Dodgers' lead and eventually won them the game and the World Series. It was the Dodgers' only title in nine World Series appearances before they moved to Los Angeles.

After leaving baseball, Sandy Amoros became ill with diabetes and battled circulatory problems that ravaged his body and led to the amputation of one of his legs. Sandy's poor health and mounting medical bills left him with very little money. Before his death on 27 June 1992, Sandy's friends spent a lot of time raising money to pay for his medical expenses. Among those who helped were old-time Brooklyn Dodgers fans, Dodgers teammates—and Yogi Berra. Yes, Yogi Berra, the very man whom Sandy had caught out in the World Series. It's plain that Yogi understood that friendship is more important than a game.

True friendship is different from the friendship the

world teaches. The world teaches a false kind of friendship that is conditional. There are strings attached. A false friend says, "If you do something for me, I will be your friend and love you. If you don't, I guess we can no longer be friends." That kind of friendship is nothing more than a game, with winners and losers.

In real, unconditional friendships there are only winners. In the 1955 World Series, Sandy Amoros was the winner and Yogi Berra was the loser. In the "Eternal Series," both Sandy and Yogi were winners. Sandy won as the receiver, and Yogi as the giver.

There is a saying that "what goes around comes around." If you are a good friend, chances are good that you will have friends. If you have been there for your friends when they needed someone, they will probably be there for you when you have problems. On the other hand, if you haven't put anything into your friendship, you probably won't get much in return.

For as long as Elizabeth could remember she had been taught that "families are forever." She had never doubted the truth of that statement—that is, until something happened that turned her life upside down.

It all started one day when her mother came to her and asked, "How would you feel if I told you I wanted to divorce your father?" Elizabeth's first reaction was, "This isn't real. It has to be a bad dream. It can't be real!" Elizabeth told her mother that she would be very hurt! The subject was dropped, but she could not get it off her mind. Her parents hadn't been happy together for years, but Elizabeth had of course hoped it would all work out.

She went to her room crying and asked God, "Aren't families forever? If they are, show me a sign." No sign or immediate answer came. In fact, a few months later, her father told her that she had better start thinking about who she wanted to live with because he and her mother were going to separate. All she could think was, "How can I

choose who to live with? I love them both so much. I love
my mother for her tenderness, and I love my father for his
quiet support." She kept asking herself, "Aren't families
forever? If so, why can't mine be?"

Irrationally, Elizabeth began to blame herself. She would
ask herself, "What did I do wrong?" And she finally concluded, "If I were a better daughter, this probably wouldn't
be happening!"

One night she had a dream. She dreamed she was lost in
a forest and was clinging to a tree for comfort. Not wanting to let go because she was so scared, Elizabeth was
approached by Christ, who said to her, "Why are you holding on to that tree? That tree cannot give you the comfort
that I can."

Crying, Elizabeth said, "Lord, I cannot let go! I cannot! I
am scared and lost. This tree will give me support!" The
Lord drew her to himself and held her, which brought her
great joy and comfort. His love was sweeter than anything
she had ever experienced. His comfort was real!

As Elizabeth awoke she found her pillow soaked with
tears. She felt that she understood the dream! The tree was
the world, which doesn't provide real comfort. No matter
how tightly she held on to it, it couldn't comfort her. She
now understood that when people turn to the Lord, they
feel a comfort and a happiness that the world can't provide. Elizabeth had experienced a taste of pure joy.

As time passed and Elizabeth continued to try to deal
with the hurt and confusion caused by her parents' sepa-
ration, she discovered another way the Lord extends comfort to us. One evening she went to the Lord in prayer, saying, "I need comfort, and you have said that the scriptures
have been written for us in these latter days. Please let me
know where to read. I really need comfort now." As she
got up from her prayer, she threw her scriptures onto her
bed. They opened to Doctrine and Covenants 78:17–18,
which reads: "Verily, verily, I say unto you, ye are little

children, and ye have not as yet understood how great blessings the Father hath in his own hands and prepared for you; and ye cannot bear all things now; nevertheless, be of good cheer, for I will lead you along. The kingdom is yours and the blessings thereof are yours, and the riches of eternity are yours." It was then that she gained a testimony of the power and comfort the Lord offers us through the scriptures.

Elizabeth also learned that friends are another source of comfort. After sitting in church one day, hurting inside over the problems with her family, she went out into the foyer. There she met a friend who asked how she was doing. As they talked, the friend sensed that things were not well. Elizabeth described the struggle she was having. The friend wisely reminded Elizabeth that she could have an eternal family of her own, and how right now through proper dating and right living she was setting out on the path to an eternal family. As they finished their conversation the friend hugged Elizabeth. At that moment she felt the same comfort and joy she had experienced in her dream.

Another source of comfort was her Church meetings. In her Laurel class they had a lesson on eternal marriage. She learned that if she desired an eternal family, she would first have to date wisely and be loving and Christlike. The lesson also helped her identify the qualities to look for in an eternal mate.

Working through this troubled time in her life, Elizabeth discovered what great comfort Heavenly Father and Jesus Christ have to offer us. She came to understand better the Savior's tender promise: "Behold, I stand at the door, and knock: if any man hear my voice, and open the door, I will come in to him, and will sup with him, and he with me" (Revelation 3:20).

Always remember that our greatest friends are Heavenly Father and Jesus. They are always available and will listen when we need them. They can always be trusted because their love is perfect.

 Max H. Molgard is an institute instructor at Salt Lake Community College. He holds a bachelor's degree in psychology and an M.Ed. degree in secondary education from Utah State University. A published author, he serves on the Church's youth curriculum writing committee. He and his wife, Bette, have six children.

17

WHAT IF . . . I CHOOSE THE RIGHT?

Todd Murdock

race yourself. I'm about to unveil the most-asked question I hear from youth today. Actually, there are several questions, but they all begin in this way: "What if . . . ?"

Some "what if" questions are legitimate and deserve legitimate answers, but far too many are asked in an attempt to justify inappropriate behavior. For example, consider the following questions I've actually been asked: "What if you go water-skiing on Sunday, but it's with your family. Is that still keeping the Sabbath Day holy?" or "What if I play poker, but I pay tithing on the money I win. Isn't that okay?" Here's an even more famous one I hear when discussing the Word of Wisdom: "What if you go to a party where there's booze, but you know you're not going to drink—just give rides to your friends who are drunk. That's okay, right?" I am not making these questions up. I've actually heard young people ask about things like that.

Such inquiries remind me of the Savior's rebuke to the Scribes and Pharisees, "Ye blind guides, who strain at a gnat, and swallow a camel; *who make yourselves appear unto men that ye would not commit the least sin, and yet ye yourselves, transgress the whole law*" (Joseph Smith Translation,

Matthew 23:21; emphasis added). In other words, sometimes we try to justify inappropriate behavior by pretending that we're living a gospel principle at the same time.

Although it is a good thing to be with your family,
water-skiing on Sundays violates the admonition to worship in a spirit of reverence. And are you going to pay
tithing on money you *lose* in a poker game? Are you sure
you're not going to drink at the party, or become involved
with other activities that lead to immorality, deception, or
anger? Why put yourself in that kind of environment? The
funny thing is, no one can answer these questions for you.
You have to answer them for yourself.

The Savior also had to deal with "what if" questions. It's
not a new form of rationalization, unique to our generation. A great example is found in the book of Luke. "And,
behold, a certain lawyer stood up, and tempted him, saying, Master, what shall I do to inherit eternal life? He said
unto him, What is written in the law? how readest thou?
And he answering said, Thou shalt love the Lord thy God
with all thy heart, and with all thy soul, and with all thy
strength, and with all thy mind; and thy neighbour as thyself. And he said unto him, Thou hast answered right: this
do, and thou shalt live. But he, willing to justify himself,
said unto Jesus, And who is my neighbour?" (Luke
10:25–29).

Did you pick up on the "what if" question asked by the
lawyer in this example? Jesus did. And immediately, the
Savior related the parable of the Good Samaritan, describing to the lawyer the grim situation of a beaten man left for
dead. Travelers on the same highway walked by the man
without rendering aid. Finally, a Samaritan stopped, bound
up the beaten man's wounds, nourished him, set him on
his own animal, and took him to an inn to be cared for. The
Savior asked the lawyer who he thought acted as a true
neighbor in the story. The reply, "He that shewed mercy on

him. Then said Jesus unto him, Go, and do thou likewise" (Luke 10:37).

The answer to the lawyer's question wasn't found in who lived closest to the needy man but in who was willing to offer compassion. That the kindly man in the parable was one of the despised Samaritans was a detail Jesus' adversaries would have noted.

Trying to live the gospel in these days has its unique challenges. However, it's not impossible. It requires the individual who is asking the "what if" question to look into his heart and examine his underlying motive. President Howard W. Hunter taught us how to do this. He said, "We are at a time in the history of the world and the growth of the Church when we must think more of holy things and act more like the Savior would expect his disciples to act. We should at every opportunity ask ourselves, 'What would Jesus do?' and then act more courageously upon the answer" (*Ensign*, November 1994, p. 87).

Six months later, President Gordon B. Hinckley stated, "This is a season to be strong. It is a time to do what is right regardless of the consequences that might follow. It is a time to be found keeping the commandments" (*Ensign*, May 1995, p. 71).

Instead of asking "what if," we should begin asking, "What would Jesus do?" I know this makes many of us cringe because the answers become obvious. Consequently, we recognize the need to change our behavior. Sometimes we fear that this reformation of action will exclude us from friends, activities, and popularity. But the Savior has promised great blessings to the obedient.

What concerns Christ is the real intent of our hearts. When we are brought to the judgment bar of the Lord, we know that we will be rewarded according to our actions on the earth and the desires of our hearts. "For I, the Lord, will judge all men according to their works, according to the desire of their hearts" (D&C 137:9). The important principle to recognize is that we can't deceive the Lord. He knows the deepest motivations of our hearts, whether we're honestly trying to live the gospel or secretly covering our sins.

At that great judgment scene we won't be able to talk our way out of poor behavior. Jesus said, "Not every one that saith unto me, Lord, Lord, shall enter into the kingdom of heaven; but he that doeth the will of my Father which is in heaven. Many will say to me in that day, Lord, Lord, have we not prophesied in thy name? and in thy name have cast out devils? and in thy name done many wonderful works? And then will I profess unto them, I never knew you: depart from me, ye that work iniquity" (Matthew 7:21–23). Can you imagine hearing at the judgment bar something like this, "Lord, Lord, did we not water-ski with our family on Sunday, did we not pay tithing on our poker winnings, and attend wild parties so that we could drive our drunken friends home, and many other wonderful works?" Whoops, that doesn't sound like a very good argument. It is important to know that the Lord will be merciful, but only if our hearts are pure.

I believe that the majority of the youth truly have pure hearts and are honestly trying to live like Christ. Many are concerned for their friends and want to help. Many are preparing to serve faithful missions and go to the temple. These are the desires of their hearts. Wonderful! Keep going, and you'll find that it's not hard to do what is right—it only takes practice.

I remember when I was younger, I played on a Little League football team. One day during practice our coach wanted to drill the first-team kick-off squad. I was asked to be on the kick-return team and run back the ball. It was like committing suicide. But I decided deep in my heart that rather than be a tackling dummy, I would run through the defense and score a touchdown. Each time I caught the ball I ran as hard as I could, but each time I was crushed by the oncoming tacklers. Once my best friend tackled me and started screaming in my ear as if I were his worst enemy. I felt tears form in my eyes. I quickly jumped up and ran back to my position so that I wouldn't be seen with watery eyes. The first team kicked off again and I caught the ball, tucked it under my right arm, and started to run. I ran up the middle and then suddenly cut to my left. I saw all the would-be tacklers try to stop and change direction, but I had caught them off guard and my blockers knocked them to the ground. All I could see was a wide open field. I ran as hard as I could, knowing I was going to score. I was so excited I started to smile. I heard one of my coaches screaming "Go! Go! Go!!! I knew you could do it!" I ran into the end zone and spiked the ball. My coach caught me in the end zone and gave me a big hug—of course, in a manly, football sort of way. I knew deep down inside my heart, I could do it. Believing that I could succeed had a lot to do with what I was able to do.

It's the same with trying to live a good life. It helps to know deep down inside that we are capable of doing so.

I know that deep inside our hearts, we really want to do what's right. At times it may seem hard, and our choices may strain our relationships with our friends, but the righteous desires of our hearts will always be rewarded.

When you walk your daily walk, and it seems that others are trying to drag you down, look to the Savior. He can give you answers to your problems, give you the strength to stand up for the Church, and help you teach your friends and set the correct example. Remember, he said, "And I say unto you, Ask, and it shall be given you; seek, and ye shall find; knock, and it shall be opened unto you. For every one that asketh receiveth; and he that seeketh findeth; and to him that knocketh it shall be opened" (Luke 11:9–11).

By asking "What would the Savior do?" or "What can I do to become more like Christ?" you will be able to make correct choices more often and resolve problems and questions that only you can answer for yourself.

Todd Murdock served a mission in Alabama and later graduated from Weber State University in communications. He teaches seminary at Brighton High School in Salt Lake City, Utah. He loves hiking and skiing. This is his second year as an EFY counselor.

18

"KNOW YE NOT THAT YE ARE THE TEMPLE OF GOD?"

Gary R. Nelson

After purchasing two new Honda motorcycles from my father's cycle shop, a metro police officer and his wife asked about a place to camp and ride for the weekend. Following directions they were given, the couple traveled thirty-two miles north of St. George to the Pine Valley Mountain campground area. Riding the two brand new cycles must have been exciting. Both bikes were decked out with the finest accessories, including ferrings, windshields, crash bars, and customized seats for two with an attached sissy bar and pad. Although the couple had not originally planned to buy two bikes, they had done so, and the officer's wife felt first-rate riding next to him on her somewhat smaller model.

After enjoying a weekend of camping in the cool fresh air alongside the pristine reservoir and streams and amidst the lush green meadows and towering ponderosa pines, the couple journeyed down the winding Pine Valley Mountain road to return home. Concerned about his wife's inexperience as a rider, the officer cautiously followed about seventy-five yards behind her. After crossing two cattle guards, the fully helmeted cyclists hit a one-mile straight stretch in the road. Tempted by the thrill and freedom of the open road, the couple cranked up their gas throttles a bit more. Riding in the lead, the officer's wife was traveling about fifty miles per hour. Unaware of the tragedy looming mere seconds ahead, she was enjoying the smooth, quiet, four-cylindered roadbike as it carried her downward. With *no warning signs* posted to reduce speed or prepare to turn, the road suddenly jagged to the left. The unsuspecting and inexperienced female cyclist was not able to negotiate the sharp turn. The heavy cycle left the shoulder of the road, and the momentum hurled her body into the protruding branches of a roadside cedar tree, killing her instantly. Her cycle crashed over the embankment onto the rocks below. One can only imagine the horror and feeling of helpless despair experienced by her husband as he witnessed the entire scene transpiring before his eyes.

The unforgettable details of that day are something I will not soon forget. The sad thing is that a simple warning sign and a more cautious driving style might have helped prevent that senseless, unfortunate loss of life. One sign limiting speed to forty miles per hour and warning of the curve now stands as a silent, poignant reminder of the past.

THE LORD HAS PROVIDED
WARNING SIGNS TO HELP US

One of the greatest comforts to the youth of today is to know that the Lord cares for you and is concerned about your temporal and spiritual welfare. Because the Savior cares so deeply for your eternal happiness, he has appointed concerned leaders to help you become familiar with the road. These divinely called leaders serve as "watchmen on the tower," and they hold up the "warning signs" that, if observed, will help you avoid injury to body or soul as you safely travel the strait and narrow path that leads back to the presence of God.

In 1990, the First Presidency published the pamphlet *For the Strength of Youth*. It contains twelve standards or "warning signs" that, if followed, will help guide you past the "polluted potholes," the "destructive detours," and the "tempting turn-outs" Satan would use to destroy you. This pamphlet is scripture to the youth of Zion. Speaking of the leaders of the Church, the Lord has said, "And whatsoever they shall speak when moved upon by the Holy Ghost shall be scripture, shall be the will of the Lord, shall be the mind of the Lord, shall be the word of the Lord, shall be the voice of the Lord, and the power of God unto salvation" (D&C 68:4).

The Lord ratified the importance of our inspired priesthood leaders when he said, "What I the Lord have spoken, I have spoken, and I excuse not myself; . . . my word shall not pass away, but shall all be fulfilled, whether by mine own voice or by the voice of my servants, it is the same" (D&C 1:38).

To emphasize the importance of this life-saving document as modern scripture from our living prophets, I encourage each of my seminary students to glue a copy of the pamphlet in the front flap of their scriptures, retaining a smaller copy for their purses or wallets.

MY BODY IS A TEMPLE OF GOD

The Lord has blessed us with temples in which we can receive sacred ordinances and make eternal covenants that will enable us to eventually come back into his presence. The house of the Lord is a special building, dedicated by his servants. It is holy. It is pure and wholesome. It is clean. One who enters worthily into God's house, to there do God's work, can feel God's Spirit. If Christ were to come today to visit this beautiful earth that he created (see Ephesians 3:9), he would come to his house, the temple. Would you and I be worthy to go see him and rejoice in his presence? The strait and narrow path leads to the temple.

Satan wants to do all in his power to see that we do not

make it to Christ's house, where families are sealed and God's children are endowed with power and great spiritual blessings. Satan is the "father of lies" (2 Nephi 9:9); the "master of sin" and "an enemy to all righteousness" (Mosiah 4:14); the great deceiver (see D&C 50:3). He is literally searching for ways to influence you to sin and would like nothing better than to raise havoc with your mission here on earth, tempting you to leave the path, in an effort to destroy you. "He goeth up and down, to and fro in the earth, seeking to destroy the souls of men . . . think[ing] to overpower your testimony in this generation" (D&C 10:27, 33). If the devil can get you to sin and break the commandments, he has won a great battle in his campaign to keep you out of the house of the Lord. Such stumbling blocks and diversions can halt our spiritual progress on earth. Mission plans and temple marriages can be forgotten and rationalized away.

One of the snares Satan uses to entrap us and pull us from the sure path is to encourage us to misuse the divine power of procreation. "The most favorite method the enemy of our souls has employed in ages past and that he will employ today is to capture souls by leading them gently, step by step, towards the greatest and most destructive sin against spiritual life—immorality, the ultimate end of self-indulgence" (Melvin J. Ballard, *New Era,* March 1984, p. 38).

The apostle Paul wrote to the Corinthian Saints: "Know ye not that ye are the temple of God, and that the Spirit of God dwelleth in you? If any man defile the temple of God, him shall God destroy; for the temple of God is holy, which temple ye are" (1 Corinthians 3:16–17).

Somebody once said, "My body is a temple, not a visitor's center, and you do not have a recommend!"

SEXUAL PURITY—THE NINTH WARNING SIGN

The ninth standard in the *For the Strength of Youth* pamphlet is sexual purity. "Our Heavenly Father has counseled that sexual intimacy should be reserved for his children within the bonds of marriage. The physical relationship between a husband and a wife can be beautiful and sacred. It is ordained of God for the procreation of children and for the expression of love within a marriage. . . . Because sexual intimacy is so sacred, the Lord requires self-control and purity before marriage as well as full fidelity after marriage"(pp. 14–15).

This is not a new standard. The prophets have always spoken out boldly on the need to keep ourselves morally clean. "That the Church's stand on morality may be understood, we declare firmly and unalterably, it is not an outworn garment, faded, old-fashioned, and threadbare. God is the same yesterday, today, and forever, and his covenants and doctrines are immutable; and when the sun grows cold and the stars no longer shine, the law of chastity will still be basic in God's world and in the Lord's church. Old values are upheld by the Church not because they are old, but rather because through the ages they have proved right" (Spencer W. Kimball, *Ensign,* November 1980, p. 96).

THE HIGH COST OF LOW LIVING

Roller skating is a sport and hobby I have enjoyed all my life. I even managed a roller rink for a few years. A favorite activity of the skaters is to "limbo." Each of the skaters tries to bend backward low enough to pass under the limbo sticks. I can still remember some of the words to the limbo song: "Limbo lower now . . . Limbo lower now . . . *How low can you go?*" Unfortunately, that is a question too many young people seem to be asking with regard to immoral behavior: "How *low* can I go in my moral relationships?"

Rather than trying to decide how *low* you will go, you need to draw a line at a *high* level. Then as you enter into the dating years you can avoid the pitfalls and mine fields of Satan. Be aware of the tactics and flattery the devil uses and *avoid* his alluring entrapments at all costs, "that [you] may recover [yourself] out of the snare of the devil" (2

Timothy 2:26). Not having a body, he would like to destroy yours and have you become miserable "like unto himself" (2 Nephi 9:9). Yes, simply speaking, Satan's snares spell S-I-N. Choose today "how high" you will go to avoid Satan. Obeying the "warning signs" will keep you safe as you travel on higher ground.

HEEDING THE WARNING AND
TRAFFIC SIGNS ALONG THE WAY

Once while driving in Ogden, Utah, I noticed that all the cars were going a different direction than I was. I actually got upset at them. *What a bunch of dumb drivers,* I thought. After traveling nearly two blocks, going the wrong way on a one-way street, I realized who the dumb one really was. Talk about embarrassing! Road signs enable us to enjoy our freedoms and they keep us safe. Let's examine some of the road warning signs we see daily. Maybe they can serve to remind us to be chaste and true.

KEEP RIGHT

You need to give heed to the warning sign to "Keep Right." Stay on the right path; be the right person; choose the right; don't become "too familiar" with those you date. Flirting, holding hands, sharing hugs should be done with discretion; you might simply choose not to participate in any of them. If your date is uncomfortable with *any* of these activities, they should be avoided.

"In dating, treat your date with respect, and expect your date to show that same respect to you" (*For the Strength of Youth,* p. 15).

YIELD

To "yield" is to move forward with caution, to stop when conditions do not permit safe access. So it is with the first kiss—*yield to the right way.* If you are not comfortable with a kiss, you should make sure your date understands that your line has been drawn here. Whether it is a peck on the cheek, or a kiss on the lips, you need to determine beforehand what you feel *safe* in doing. Maybe you could hold out, as I did. I did not kiss my wife until we had been sealed in the temple. (Of course, she wasn't my wife before that!) If thoughts of expressing open affections "scare the heaven" out of you, may I suggest you exchange a "high-five" with your date at the doorstep. This simple ceremony can save you from embarrassing and difficult situations.

Actions like flirting, holding hands, and giving hugs and kisses lead to greater intimacies that should be fully realized only in the intimate bonds of marriage, and not be shared thoughtlessly or carelessly before marriage. "Flee also youthful lusts: but follow righteousness, faith, charity, peace, with them that call on the Lord out of a pure heart" (2 Timothy 2:22).

"Properly understood, the scriptures and the prophets counsel us to be virtuous not because romantic love is bad, but precisely because romantic love is so good. It is not only good, it is pure, precious, and even sacred and holy. For that very reason, one of Satan's cheapest and dirtiest tricks is to make profane that which is sacred" (Bruce C. Hafen, *Ensign,* October 1982, p. 66).

If kissing is not restricted or curbed, it can encourage you to become more passionate and intimate. Heavy kissing—"making out," spooning, or engaging in French kissing—should be avoided at all costs. Even the ancient Old Testament prophet Isaiah may well have been describing this type of kissing behavior in Isaiah 57:1–4. President Spencer W. Kimball also warned against this type of kissing. "What is miscalled the 'soul kiss' is an abomination and stirs passions to the eventual loss of virtue. Even if timely courtship justifies the kiss it should be a clean, decent, sexless one like the kiss between mother and son, or father and daughter. . . . If the 'soul kiss' with its passion were eliminated from dating there would be an immediate upswing in chastity and honor, with fewer illegitimate babies, fewer unwed mothers, fewer forced marriages, fewer unhappy people" (*The Teachings of Spencer W. Kimball* [Salt Lake City: Bookcraft, 1982], p. 281).

 ### DO NOT ENTER

Danger looms beyond the "Do Not Enter" sign. These are forbidden sexual paths. The next steps along the path of sexual intimacy are those sister sins of necking and petting. These seem to be interrelated; it is difficult to determine where one ends and the other begins.

President Kimball stated: "With the absence of the 'soul kiss,' necking would be greatly reduced. The younger sister of petting, it [necking] should be totally eliminated. Both are abominations in their own right" (*The Teachings of Spencer W. Kimball,* p. 281).

Necking, as I choose to define it, is moving from kissing on the lips to kissing around the neck. Petting is the actual touching and stimulation of yours or another person's body parts. Elder Richard G. Scott has declared, "Any sexual intimacy outside of the bonds of marriage—and I emphasize that means any involvement of the sacred, private parts of the body—is a sin and is forbidden by God" (*Ensign,* May 1991, p. 34).

President Kimball stated: "Who would say that he or she who pets has not become lustful, has not become passionate? Is it not this most abominable practice that God rebuked in his modern reiteration of the Ten Commandments: 'Thou shalt not . . . commit adultery . . . *nor do anything like unto it'* (D&C 59:6). What, may I ask you, is like unto adultery if it is not petting?" (*Ensign,* November 1980, p. 96).

The Apostle Paul added, "It is good for a man *not to touch a woman"* (1 Corinthians 7:1). Supporting the warning sign of "Do Not Enter" and the avoidance of the acts of necking and petting, Paul further admonished us to "Touch not; taste not; handle not" (Colossians 2:21).

Our latter-day leaders have counseled us: "Never treat your date as an object to be used for your own lustful desires or ego. Improper physical contact can cause a loss of self-control. Always stay in control of yourself and your physical feelings. . . . The Lord specifically forbids certain behaviors, including all sexual relations before marriage, petting, sex perversion (such as homosexuality, rape, and incest), masturbation, or preoccupation with sex in thought, speech, or action" (*For the Strength of Youth,* p. 15).

NO U-TURN

NO U-TURN

Once a couple has slipped to the levels of necking, petting, and finally fornication (going all the way), it is very difficult to return to just holding hands or to stop the immoral process.

Let me illustrate the danger that is involved with an example of the roller coaster. I love roller coasters. I like the thrill of the ride, the sudden turns, the wind rushing through my hair, and the challenge of riding the entire course with hands outstretched. Let's say that your car has gotten almost to the top of the first big hill and then you decide that you want off the ride. Do you think the operator will respond to your pleas and stop the ride? Ridiculous! Now that you have gotten that far, the rest of the ride is inevitable. The following graphic shows what happens. The idea for this was first shared with me years ago by a friend and colleague, Gary Poll. It is called the "Passion Profile." Although I have changed some things, the basic design is as Gary originally conceived it. Notice that flirting, holding hands, hugging, kissing, heavy kissing, necking, petting, and fornication are arranged on a semi-circle or arch in equal increments. Can you see the

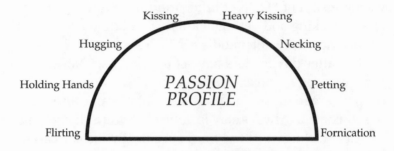

roller coaster arch and track? As you move past flirting, holding hands, hugging, and kissing, you find yourself suddenly at the top of the arch. Where have you drawn the line? How far will you go? As you move downward, the acts of necking, petting, and fornication are encountered suddenly. Because of the roller coaster effect, things happen in rapid sequence. Defenses are let down, the heat of passion is lit. Be aware of the immorality predators. They seek to obscure all the warning signs, and soon tire of one roller coaster, seeking more thrills and satisfaction on another, for they can never be satisfied.

The Lord's counsel on this subject has always been the same: "Flee fornication. . . . He that committeth fornication sinneth against his own body. What? know ye not that your body is the temple of the Holy Ghost which is in you, which ye have of God, and ye are not your own? For ye are bought with a price: therefore glorify God in your body, and in your spirit, which are God's" (1 Corinthians 6:18–20).

Elder ElRay L. Christianson quoted the First Presidency of the Church on this matter when he said: "'The doctrine of this Church is that sexual sin, the illicit sexual relationship of men and women stands in its enormity next to murder. The Lord has drawn no essential distinction between fornication, adultery, and harlotry or prostitution. . . . You youth of Zion,' they pleaded, 'you cannot associate in illicit sex relationship, which is fornication, and escape the judgments and punishments of the Lord which he has declared against this sin. The day of reckoning will come just as certainly as night follows day'" (in Conference Report, October 1959, pp. 69–70).

BE YE CLEAN THAT BEAR THE VESSELS OF THE LORD

Speaking to the Nephites on the American continent, the resurrected Christ said, "be ye clean that bear the vessels of the Lord" (3 Nephi 20:41).

For those of you who may have already had a wreck on your "morality motorcycle," there is hope after the crash and the burn. Although the repentance process is painful and difficult, it is nevertheless possible and worth it.

To those of you who have not been involved in sexual immorality, continue to strengthen your resolve, commitments, and sacred covenants. The morally clean way of life is the better life. Believe me, it is worth it. You can do it. Keep your body sacred and clean. Heed the "warning signs." They will keep you safe on the path that will return you to the presence of Heavenly Father. "Know ye not that ye are the temple of God?"

Gary R. Nelson teaches seminary in St. George, Utah, and has been a seminary principal, travel coordinator, insurance agent, roller rink manager, motorcycle salesman, and taxi driver. A former collegiate football and tennis player, Gary was a sports writer for the *Daily Spectrum,* and continues to enjoy all sports. He and his wife, Christine, have seven children.

19

LEGENDARY LEADERSHIP

Lisa Heckmann Olsen

Peach fuzz. Of all the names that the high school boys created for me, *peach fuzz* was the one that stuck. As a teenager I battled a pile of natural curly hair. Even my mom shared my frustration. Once she pulled me over to the ironing board, laid my hair down, and ran a hot iron over it. But nothing changed. I was doomed to look like human Velcro. Every night, hoping my hair would magically straighten, I twisted it into a bun. In the mornings when I woke up disappointed that my hair had not relaxed, I would roll it back into a bun on the top of my head or pull it into a braid. In addition to my unmanageable hair, I had to wear glasses and braces. Believing that all popular girls looked a certain way, I began to isolate myself socially. I never dated, mostly because I lacked the confidence to develop friendships.

One thing I wanted more than to date was to be a student leader. Desperate to be involved, I ran for office twice in junior high and four times in high school. My name never made it past the primary elections. After I had run and lost for six years, some of the students who were elected to various offices noticed how much I wanted to be involved and asked me to help. I did have something they

150

needed: I was an artist who could decorate for dances. I was flattered when they first asked. I remember thinking, "They *need* me." It was the best feeling in the world!

At the end of my sophomore year, I was asked to be head artist for the junior prom. We started plans immediately to create a memorable evening. Around the theme "Somewhere in Time" with a Camelot-type twist, we constructed a dungeon, a castle, a huge, fire-breathing dragon, and a knight on a white horse getting ready to attack the dragon. I had the best job of all—to create a forest. A week before the prom I began to paint a mural on the enormous windows of the commons, the area where the dance was to be held. The day before the prom, my father helped me assemble a forest in front of the mural. We spread fresh bark on the ground and arranged about twenty-five trees on the bark. We put stuffed deer, foxes, and other animals in the setting, along with a real waterfall. All of our creations came together! Individually and collectively we were proud. As I stood admiring the effect of what I had helped create, I hoped desperately that someone would want to take me to this dance—but no one asked.

At eight o'clock the night of the dance, the junior class president found me and nervously asked, "Lis, I hate to ask you, but I can't find a custodian. Can you vacuum the commons before the dance starts?" With only one square left to vacuum, I glanced at the couples who had started to arrive. The girls were beautiful in their formals, and the guys (sigh) looked so handsome in their tuxedos. Just then my favorite and very dramatic English teacher, Mrs. Oldroyd, touched me on the arm and said, "Dear, you need to run along and get ready for the dance!" "Um, I'm not going to the dance," I answered. She threw her hands up and said, "If I had only known!"

I hurried home, threw myself on my bed, and cried. Mom found me, put my head in her lap, and promised that my time to date would come later. Empty and rejected, I did not believe her. The phone rang. It was Mrs. Oldroyd. "Lisa, put on a Sunday dress, Scott's on his way right now to take you to the prom!"

I couldn't believe it! Her son, Scott, was a senior and a popular leader in our school. When his mom told him I wasn't going to the dance after all my work, Scott took action. Wearing his Sunday suit, he came to the door, grinned, and handed me an unexpected orchid corsage. (*How did he find one at this hour?* I remember thinking.) We made it to the last hour of the prom. For me, that prom turned into one of the most memorable events in my high school experience. A "knight in shining armor" actually took me to the dance.

I now teach at that same school, and I serve as the adviser to the student government. I want my outstanding young leaders to understand what it feels like to be left out when you want desperately to be included. So I remind them that all teenagers have an intense desire to belong and that it is vital to make everyone you serve feel important. The Lord's own admonition is to "remember the worth of souls is great in the sight of God" (D&C 18:10). Whether you are a school officer, Laurel class president, teachers quorum secretary, drama club vice president, or seminary council member, God depends on you to send this message to his children.

I suggest you ask yourself three questions to help evaluate your performance as a leader: Do you serve according to gospel principles? Do you serve with understanding and love? and, Do you serve selflessly?

SERVE ACCORDING TO GOSPEL PRINCIPLES

President Spencer W. Kimball spoke of Jesus Christ as a leader: "Jesus operated from a base of fixed principles or truths rather than making up the rules as he went along. Thus, his leadership style was not only correct, but also constant. So many secular leaders today are like chameleons; they change their hues and views to fit the situation—which only tends to confuse associates and followers who cannot be certain what course is being pursued. Jesus said several times, 'Come, follow me.' His was a program of 'do what I do,' rather than 'do what I say'" (*Teachings of Spencer W. Kimball* [Salt Lake City: Bookcraft, 1982], p. 481).

Alma the Younger, a very dynamic leader in the Book of Mormon, is both a positive and a negative example of "do what I do." Before his conversion, he is described as "a very wicked and an idolatrous man. And he was a man of many words, and did speak much flattery to the people; therefore he led many of the people to do after the manner of his iniquities. And he became a great hinderment to the prosperity of the church of God; stealing away the hearts of the people; causing much dissension among the people; giving a chance for the enemy of God to exercise his power over them" (Mosiah 27:8–9).

In this situation Alma the Younger's poor example pulled people away from the Church. Alma was obviously a charismatic person and very influential. He used flattery, perhaps phrases like, "This will make you feel good," "This will make you popular," "It's okay because everyone else is doing it," words spoken so smoothly he was able to entice people to follow him into iniquity. (Have you heard of this happening at your high school?)

After a life-changing experience with an angel and a long process of repentance (about eight years later he was ready to serve his mission), Alma the Younger became a positive example. Having acquired the Spirit, he used his persuasive powers to convert people to the Church. "Now [the sons of Mosiah and Alma] were desirous that salvation should be declared to every creature, for they could not bear that any human soul should perish; yea, even the very thoughts that any soul should endure endless torment did cause them to quake and tremble. And thus did the Spirit of the Lord work upon them, for they were the very vilest of sinners. And the Lord saw fit in his infinite mercy to spare them; nevertheless they suffered much anguish of soul because of their iniquities, suffering much and fearing that they should be cast off forever" (Mosiah 28:3–4).

I am frustrated when I watch student leaders who are members of the Church choose to behave in ways that are contrary to gospel principles. They seem to be unaware that regardless of the type of example they set, they are likely to be followed, just as Alma the Younger was. Leaders set the standard to follow. Youth are easily swayed by positive and negative leadership: "Many people, and particularly many of our youth, live a 'tumbleweed' existence. They tend to follow leadership which is dominant and powerful, regardless of whether it is right or wrong. They want to know what the other 'kids' are doing. What kind of sweaters are they wearing? What kind of shoes? Are the dresses long or short, tight or flaring? Do the leader girls wear their hair short, boyish or windswept, in pony tails or Italian or French styles? Do the boys preen before mirrors with their ducktail haircuts, their crewcuts and Mohawks, flattops and beatles, or hair dropped over the forehead?" (Spencer W. Kimball, *The Miracle of Forgiveness* [Salt Lake City: Bookcraft, 1969], p. 234).

I have seen both types of leadership. Recently a group of students started a new tradition, a cheer, at our school. It seemed harmless in the beginning but soon got out of control. Unfortunately, this cheer, the Lion Hunt, did not reflect the high standards of the majority of the student body. Each year a student was chosen to be the leader of the cheer. The leader would call out a phrase, and the student body would echo the phrase. Soon vulgar or offensive things about the opposing team or rude and demeaning things about student body members became a part of the Lion Hunt. One year a member of our student council was chosen to be the Lion Hunt leader. The great tragedy was that he honestly could not see how he was compromising himself as a leader by promoting that type of thing. Ultimately, he was removed from his office because the cheer meant more to him than supporting the people he led.

Last year a group of outstanding youth came forward. Tired of the cheer and determined to show the community that this was not representative of the entire student body, these concerned youth formed a club. It was called the "Thunder Club," a huge, dynamic spirit club. These students, more than 500 of them the first year, all signed contracts promising positive school spirit. They sat together at games and cheered with the cheerleaders. They dressed up in strange matching outfits complete with funky striped orange and blue knee socks. And their spirit didn't stop there: If there was garbage, they would pick it up. If there was graffiti, they would report it or clean it up. Their positive influence is being felt throughout the entire school as they encourage others to "do as I do."

SERVE WITH UNDERSTANDING AND LOVE

President Ezra Taft Benson spoke of the importance of loving those you serve. "A love of people is essential to effective leadership. Do you love those whom you work with? Do you realize the worth of souls is great in the sight of God (see D&C 18:10)? Do you have faith in youth? Do you find yourself praising their virtues, commending them for their accomplishments? Or do you have a critical attitude toward them because of their mistakes?" (*The Teachings of Ezra Taft Benson* [Salt Lake City: Bookcraft, 1988], p. 370).

Sometimes it's difficult to love others when you feel they are so different from you. One of my favorite passages of scripture compares the Church to the human body and points out how each part is vital to the whole. "For the body is not one member, but many. If the foot shall say,

Because I am not the hand, I am not of the body; is it therefore not of the body? And if the ear shall say, Because I am
not the eye, I am not of the body; is it therefore not of the
body? If the whole body were an eye, where were the hearing? If the whole were hearing, where were the smelling?
But now hath God set the members every one of them in
the body, as it hath pleased him. And if they were all one
member, where were the body? But now are they many
members, yet but one body. And the eye cannot say unto
the hand, I have no need of thee: nor again the head to the
feet, I have no need of you. Nay, much more those members of the body, which seem to be more feeble, are necessary: And those members of the body, which we think to
be less honourable, upon these we bestow more abundant
honour; and our uncomely parts have more abundant
comeliness. For our comely parts have no need: but God
hath tempered the body together, having given more abundant honour to that part which lacked: That there should
be no schism in the body; but that the members should
have the same care one for another. *And whether one mem-*
ber suffer, all the members suffer with it; or one member be hon-
oured, all the members rejoice with it" (1 Corinthians 12:14–26,
emphasis added).

It is the same with those we serve; we must work to
understand them and love them. Each year our student
leaders host a lip-sync contest, "Friday Nite Live." People
spend hours making up the skits and practicing. Alumni
from our school serve as the judges, and cash prizes are
given for the winning skits. Last year we had an awesome
event planned. We carefully marked off an area in front of
the stage so the performers would have room to jump
down into the audience. When the contest began, a few
students took down the barriers and started to rock the ris-
ers that served as the stage. It obviously interfered with the
performance, and as a teacher I was annoyed. Three times
I told these students to "knock it off." I was very frustrated

that they wouldn't listen to my demands. Courtney, the student body president, watched, and when I was ready to go back a fourth time, she wanted to try. I stood back and listened to her. She first introduced herself and then asked the disruptive students how she could help make their evening more enjoyable. They said that they just wanted to be closer to the stage, so they could see better. Courtney asked me if we could move the barriers a little closer; I agreed, with the understanding that the students would leave the stage alone. Then in a very gentle manner as she was about to leave, Courtney just mentioned that it was difficult for the participants to perform their lip-syncs if the stage was being rocked. It worked! When people were able to get closer to the stage, the problem was solved; they didn't interrupt. What was the difference between our two approaches? I wanted those students to do what I said, and Courtney followed Christ's example of being a listening leader. Because Christ loved others with a perfect love, he could listen and resolve concerns without being condescending.

I have also watched my students love handicapped students and work to make them feel important. Willie was one of the recipients of this great attention. Although mentally handicapped, Willie was one of the most outgoing students in our school. He was a very active member of the Thunder Club and double dated with the student leaders (he went to every date dance the school sponsored). When it came time for nominations for "most preferred," my student government excitedly announced to me that Willie had been nominated. Before final elections, a huge poster with all the nominees was hung in the commons. I have never seen such excitement. When Willie discovered his name on the list, he couldn't believe it! The officers made a fuss over him, congratulating him. Willie even asked them to save the poster so he could hang it in his room when the elections were over. Willie won "most preferred"

by a large margin. When his name was announced at the
dance, and he was standing there with his two handsome
and very popular attendants, the officers were the ones
who cheered the loudest. He grinned and grinned and
grinned. Willie wrote in his paragraph for the senior aca-
demic honors booklet that for him the most memorable
event in high school was to be elected "most preferred." I
was grateful for sincere students who made him feel so
loved and important.

SERVE SELFLESSLY

Leaders are often in the spotlight and may sometimes
forget their mission. As leaders our needs must become
second to those of the people we serve. President Kimball
reminded us how the Savior served in this manner: "The
Savior's leadership was selfless. He put himself and his
own need second and ministered to others beyond the call
of duty, tirelessly, lovingly, effectively. So many of the problems in the world today spring from selfishness and self-
centeredness in which too many make harsh demands of
life and others in order to meet their demands. This is a
direct reversal of the principles and practices pursued so
perfectly by the perfect example of leadership, Jesus of
Nazareth" (*The Teachings of Spencer W. Kimball*, p. 482).

As the Savior hung on the cross at the end of his mortal
mission, he still maintained the godly ability to put the
needs of others above his own. Three women came to comfort him; Mary (his mother), Mary's sister, and Mary
Magdalene. He was worried about those he loved, the very
people he served, and in particular his mother. "When
Jesus therefore saw his mother, and the disciple standing
by, whom he loved, he saith unto his mother, Woman,
behold thy son! Then saith he to the disciple, Behold thy
mother! And from that hour that disciple took her unto his
own home" (John 19:26–27). When the Savior was in the
greatest need of comfort, he reached out to comfort others.

The Stars Assembly is one of the most popular programs at our school. Many talented students try out, but ultimately only fifteen acts are chosen. Amy, the student body secretary, was a talented dancer who had looked forward since the ninth grade to performing in this assembly. When her name was posted as one of the acts she was thrilled! She listened to congratulations, but she also heard the disappointment of students who hadn't made it. The next day Amy came to visit me; she wanted her name removed from the list of performers. She wanted someone else to have the opportunity because, as she put it, all year she had had many opportunities to perform in front of the student body as an officer! I was very impressed by her selflessness and her desire to give someone else a chance.

I have witnessed service miracles at our school. I have watched students donate enormous amounts of money for Sub-for-Santa projects. Last year they raised over $6,000 and helped more than fifteen families. This year the student body raised $4,000 for the family of a former student who had died of cancer. After his death the parents were left with large hospital bills, which our students' donations helped to pay.

But my favorite miracle involved a student named Jason. Jason had a heart disease and needed a transplant. When the student body officers, seminary council, club officers, and other leaders in the school found out about the need, they combined their efforts and raised $20,000 (three private businesses matched the funds with an additional $60,000). Jason received his new heart. When Jason graduated, his classmates gave him a standing ovation; they were a part of his miracle. Service will bring the greatest rewards of all your activities. As we learn to put others first, our lives will be filled with peace and great joy.

In any type of leadership, you have a sacred trust from God to help his children feel loved and important. Your adult leaders have great faith in you. President Kimball

declared, "Church members have great leadership potential. You [student officers] are born leaders. Your patriarchal blessings will designate most of you as of Ephraim,
the natural leaders. You must take your stance—you must
assume your responsibility—you must measure up" (*The
Teachings of Spencer W. Kimball,* p. 476). I vividly recall my
own Knight-in-Armor experience and the leadership
opportunities that followed. May you have the same effect
on those you serve.

Lisa Heckmann Olsen teaches and serves as
the student government adviser at Timpview
High School in Utah. She served a mission in
Geneva, Switzerland, and has worked for several years in the EFY program. She loves painting, shopping, making stained glass, and playing with her pet snake, Rachid. Lisa and her
husband, Brent, have one son.

20

PRAYER: THE NEXT BEST THING TO BEING THERE

Vickey Pahnke

What is prayer? When do we pray? How do we pray? Where do we pray? Why is prayer so important? These are pretty basic questions—and important ones. Prayer has to be real, or it cannot be a meaningful part of your life.

Have you experienced a time when a prayer has been answered immediately? That's an awesome experience. You have also probably spent time on your knees only to feel that your prayers weren't heard. Some of your prayers have been big ones, and others were for tiny blessings. Sometimes there are even prayers that make you giggle.

Be honest. Hasn't there been a time in your family when someone said a prayer that made you want to laugh? I figure Heavenly Father has a perfect sense of humor and that he gets an occasional chuckle from the prayers we utter. Consider a couple of mine:

Several years ago we had invited some close friends over for dinner. We had known this couple for years, attending the same ward and frequently socializing with them. They had been in our home many times. So imagine my surprise when we bowed our heads for my husband to ask the blessing on the meal, and we heard him say, "And we are thankful the . . . the . . . umm . . . we are glad that . . . umm . . . we are glad our friends could join us for dinner."

I was embarrassed, but probably not as much as my husband. Aghh! The dreaded mental block! As soon as the "amens" had been said, we all burst into laughter. Another memory was added to our "giggle prayers" list.

My mother tells the story of a "special" prayer I once said at the table. No more than four years old, I loved being our family spokesman. With company over for dinner, I was permitted to say the prayer, and I closed by saying something like, "We are thankful for our friends and hope they will come back soon so that Mommy will make another nice meal."

I honestly don't remember what we had for dinner every night, but we certainly didn't starve. Mom came from a Virginia family, steeped in southern hospitality, so cooking was high on her list of priorities. We aren't sure if our friends realized that, though. Thank goodness moms forgive . . . and teach us, so that our prayers evolve into more meaningful communication!

From the mouths of our prophets and from the scriptures, we can learn much about the "what," "when," "how," "why," and "where" of prayer.

1. *What is prayer?* Elder Bruce R. McConkie explains that "to pray is to speak with God, either vocally or by forming the thoughts involved in the mind." He further says that perfect prayers are those that are inspired, in which the Spirit reveals the words that should be used (see *Mormon Doctrine*, 2d ed. [Salt Lake City: Bookcraft, 1966], p. 581). We speak, we listen, we create a real and meaningful relationship.

Elder Neal A. Maxwell helpfully explains that "petitioning in prayer has taught me, again and again, that the vault of heaven with all its blessings is to be opened only by a combination lock. One tumbler falls when there is faith, a second when there is personal righteousness; the third and final tumbler falls only when what is sought is, in God's judgment—not ours—right for us. Sometimes we pound on the vault door for something we want very much and wonder why the door does not open. We would be very spoiled children if that vault door opened any more easily than it does" (*New Era*, April 1978, p. 6).

I think of the painting of Christ standing at a door that has no handle on his side, symbolizing that he won't force his way into our lives. But we can swing the door open wide by means of our sincere prayers. We can witness miracles, for "prayer is the instrument of miracles" (Marion G. Romney, *Ensign*, November 1984, p. 27).

Matthew 7:7 teaches, "Ask, and it shall be given you; seek, and ye shall find; knock, and it shall be opened unto you." This is prayer!

2. *When should we pray?* According to Alma 13:28 we should "pray continually, that ye may not be tempted." Considering the world we live in, and the temptations and problems that fall on all of us from time to time, it sounds like a pretty good line of defense to keep a prayer in our hearts *all the time*. No one else may know the difficulties or heartaches we suffer, but God does. You will be blessed with increased strength against the adversary and a renewed resolve to hang on if you continually pray for what is needed.

Elder Howard W. Hunter told us, "If prayer is only a spasmodic cry at the time of crisis, then it is utterly selfish, and we come to think of God as a repairman or a service agency to help us only in our emergencies" (*Ensign*, November 1977, p. 52).

During our prayers is a time to share all our feelings and all our desires and all our thanks with Father. Just as I like to hear my children thank me for the things I have done for them, so Father in Heaven likes to hear our thanks. This is not because an acknowledgment is needed, but because our expression of thanks allows us to focus on the good things that we often take for granted.

Pray when you want to thank him. Pray when you need to petition him. Pray when you are lonely or concerned or even bored. Pray "always" in your heart. At the very least, pray morning and evening and at mealtimes. Then progress until you can do as the Savior taught, "always to pray, and not faint" (Luke 18:1).

3. *How do we pray?* The Savior taught us the manner of prayer we should follow in what we call the Lord's prayer. Matthew 6:9–13 records the words of the Son to his Father. The example is simple, heartfelt, loving, and personal, just as you and I should address our Father. Our aim ought to be to establish a personal relationship with Heavenly Father, so that our prayers can be offered "in faith, nothing wavering" (James 1:6).

Elder H. Burke Peterson suggested what I call the "prayer rock plan." Find a good-sized rock, wash it, and place it under your pillow. If you climb into bed at night without saying your prayers, your head will hit the rock. That will remind you to get down on your knees and visit with Father. After you have finished, place the rock on the floor by your bed. In the morning your feet will come down on the rock. That serves as your reminder to say your morning prayers. It might seem like a simple tactic, but if it helps to form the habit of saying prayers, it's a great plan!

Friends who investigate the Church are taught to pray to the Father, to thank him, to ask him for specific blessings, and to close in the name of Jesus Christ. No one says, "Be eloquent." Father doesn't expect us to use words that make us uncomfortable. He just wants us to talk to him . . . and then to listen for his reply. When you speak on the phone with a friend, you talk and you listen. You ask questions and you give answers. You *communicate.* And there you have it: to have effectual prayers, communicate with Father in Heaven.

From time to time we have the opportunity to fast and pray. By abstaining from physical nourishment, we allow our focus to be on the nourishing of our spirit. Christ exemplified this in a great way when he went into the desert for forty days and forty nights (see Matthew 4:2). If you feel the desire to get closer to God, if you seek answers to special prayers or feel the need for extra spiritual strength, consider choosing to fast in preparing to pray— not because you *have* to, but because you *want* to.

4. *Why pray?* We pray because we have been told to. Alma 37:37 says, "Counsel with the Lord in all thy doings." Thinking logically, why would we choose to go through life—or any part of it—on our own when we could have help along the way? President Marion G. Romney reminded us, "No divine commandment has been more frequently repeated than the commandment to pray in the name of the Lord Jesus Christ" (*Ensign,* November 1979, p. 16). A careful look at Matthew 7:7–11 will reveal the comfort prayer can bring to us. Father wants to give us good things, but we have to ask.

We pray because we need to. We might otherwise go in a direction contrary to that which is best for us. Without prayer, we might go through problems we could avoid. We may emerge from life's darkest moments as much better people when prayer is our companion. Things can get rough for us, young friend. Don't try to go it alone.

President Spencer W. Kimball taught us, "Sometimes ideas flood our mind as we listen after our prayers. Sometimes feelings press upon us. A spirit of calmness assures us that all will be well. But always, if we have been honest and earnest, we will experience a good feeling—a feeling of warmth for our Father in Heaven and a sense of his love for us" (*Ensign,* October 1981, p. 5).

Prayer does not provide a quick fix or represent a short-

cut in a world of problems and complexities, but it can be a
spiritual bandage when we need to heal; it is a sure way to
obtain truth in a world of falsehoods; it is a means of
becoming more humble and teachable, so that our lives
conform more to the Lord's will. That makes us happy.
And it makes Heavenly Father happy.

5. *Where do we pray?* This is a given. Pray anywhere and
everywhere. Pray while you're driving or bicycling, standing in an elevator or waiting in a checkout line. Pray in the
halls of school (and not only before a big test). Pray standing or sitting or kneeling. Pray when you are working and
when you are playing. Pray when you are prompted and
pray when you are tempted—particularly when you don't
feel like it at all. Pray wherever you are.

Several years ago I was in Las Vegas for an Education
Days program. One member of our teaching team shared
a great idea for praying over meals in a public place. He
said he always gets a "Mormon headache" before beginning to eat. Placing his hand on his forehead, he bows his
head, offers a quick thanks and blessing, and then pro-
ceeds with his meal. I thought this was an effective way to
offer a blessing without being too conspicuous or calling
undue attention to yourself. The Savior suggested that
"hypocrites . . . love to pray standing in the synagogues
and in the corners of the streets, that they may be seen of
men" (Matthew 6:5). He teaches us to pray privately.

Prayer is so important. The bigger part prayer plays in
our lives, the better quality of life we will have. Have you
ever made a deal with God? You know, bargaining that if
he will just do this one thing for you, you will *never* . . . or if
he will get you out of this spot, you will *always* . . . whatever. Using prayer to bargain with the Lord reveals a lack
of understanding of the majesty and sacredness of this
divine communication. Seek *his* will. Do *his* bidding. "Seek
ye first the kingdom of God, and his righteousness; and all
these things shall be added unto you" (Matthew 6:33).

Concentrate for clarity in prayers. If you have ever wandered mentally when praying, you may have found yourself thinking about some new student at school, or that test coming up, or a hot fudge sundae, or how you wish your acne would go away. All this while you are attempting to call upon Heavenly Father.

How would you feel if you were deep in conversation with your dad and, right in midsentence, he were to turn his head away and dreamily start rambling about this new Porsche he saw today, or a problem at work that is bugging him? He shakes it off, apologizes, and you begin again. But moments later, he gets a blank look on his face and begins babbling about his favorite football team. You'd probably worry about the poor man—and be frustrated by his inattention.

When we pray, we are speaking to our Father. Don't you suppose he would like us to pay attention and really *communicate?* This might include expanding our vocabulary. If you have gotten into the habit of saying the same things in the same way, you might improve the effectiveness of your prayers by expressing your feelings in new ways. Imagine how much better your relationship could be if you tried talking to God as though he were your best friend. Envision him, reach for him, speak from your heart. Just as we guard against repeating ourselves in ordinary conversation, we should try to avoid using repetitive wording in our prayers.

Prayer packs a powerful punch. God is not too busy to pay attention to us when we have lost our keys or can't get to sleep. He is available anytime, for any reason, for *you.*

He knows and loves you, my friend. I know there are loved ones, leaders, and others to help you with your life's plan and problems. But there is *no one*—NO ONE—who loves you more than Heavenly Father does. No one understands you so well or can guide you more completely.

Pray. Get to know him better. Plead for more direction. Pray for help in going home to him again.

You are cared about more than you can imagine. You are known through and through. You have forgotten for a moment, but you have shared a wonderful relationship with your Father in Heaven. *Pray.* He will hear you. And he will answer you. You *can* feel his nearness. You cannot be with him just now. But prayer is the next best thing to being there.

Vickey Pahnke holds bachelor's and master's degrees in communication from Brigham Young University. She works as a songwriter, vocalist, and producer. A popular speaker, she loves mountains, laughter, kids of all ages, music, food, teaching, cooking, and traveling—but mostly she loves being a mom. Vickey and her husband, Bob, have four children.

21

LET US PUT ON THE ARMOR OF LIGHT

————•◦•————

Todd B. Parker

How did David slay Goliath? A rock to the head? Yes, but why was David able to hit Goliath in the head? Goliath's forehead was the one vulnerable spot where he was not protected by his armor. Scholars estimate Goliath stood between nine and eleven feet tall and wore a coat of armor weighing over 200 pounds. His spearhead alone weighed twelve pounds. Just as David slew an evil giant by hitting him where his armor failed to protect him, Satan tries to slay spiritual giants by hitting them in places unprotected by spiritual armor.

The apostle Paul knew of Satan's tactic when he instructed the Ephesians to protect themselves with spiritual armor. Said he: "Wherefore take unto you the whole armour of God, that ye may be able to withstand in the evil day, and having done all, to stand. Stand therefore, having your loins girt about with truth, and having on the breastplate of righteousness; And your feet shod with the preparation of the gospel of peace; Above all, taking the shield of faith, wherewith ye shall be able to quench all the fiery darts of the wicked. And take the helmet of salvation, and the sword of the Spirit, which is the word of God" (Ephesians 6:13–17).

Elder Harold B. Lee once explained the symbolism associated with this armor. He specified four areas that are favorite targets of the adversary: "We have four parts of the body that . . . [are] the most vulnerable to the powers of darkness. The loins, typifying virtue, chastity; the heart, typifying our conduct; our feet, our goals or objectives in life; and finally, our head, our thoughts" (Speech delivered at Brigham Young University, November 9, 1954).

Let's examine each of the four areas that Satan targets and decide how to best use the armor to protect ourselves.

CHASTITY

Elder Lee suggested that the loins (the part of the body where our reproductive organs are located) are a symbol of chastity and virtue. What influences in the world attack this section of our armor?

Elder Gene R. Cook once had a conversation with a rock music star on a plane in which the singer informed Elder Cook that his music was "calculated to drive the kids to have sex." He also said he was glad it was now possible to make music videos in which sex could be more explicitly depicted. He saw this as a way to have a greater impact on youth and to make more money. Elder Cook was dismayed that while he was traveling the world to teach virtue to the youth, misguided and selfish individuals were working to undo all the good he had done (see *13 Lines of Defense: Living the Law of Chastity*, talk on cassette [Salt Lake City: Deseret Book, 1991]).

It seems that Satan targets virtue in young people perhaps more than the other three areas. Why? The Lord states: "For strait is the gate, and narrow the way that leadeth unto the exaltation and continuation of the lives, and few there be that find it, because ye receive me not in the world neither do ye know me. But if ye receive me in the world, then shall ye know me, and shall receive your exaltation; that where I am ye shall be also. This is eternal lives—to know the only wise and true God, and Jesus Christ, whom he hath sent. I am he. Receive ye, therefore, my law. Broad is the gate, and wide the way that leadeth to the deaths; and many there are that go in thereat, because they receive me not, neither do they abide in my law" (D&C 132:22–25).

Commenting on these verses, Elder Joseph Fielding Smith explained, "What does the Lord mean by 'the deaths'? . . . He means they enter into the world-to-come 'separately and singly,' and they have no continuation of the 'lives,' no increase. That is death. They don't go on; *they come to an end as far as that progression is concerned.* The Lord calls it 'the deaths,' . . . he has reached the end—not the end of his life but *the end of increase.*

"The gift promised to those who receive this covenant of marriage and *remain faithful to the end,* that they shall 'have no end,' means that they shall have the power of *eternal increase. Only those who have this power will truly 'know the only wise and true God, and Jesus Christ, whom he hath sent.'* Others may *see* the Lord and may be *instructed by him,* but they will not truly *know* him or his Father unless they become *like* them" (*Doctrines of Salvation,* comp. Bruce R. McConkie, 3 vols. [Salt Lake City: Bookcraft, 1954–55], 2:64; italics in original).

The reason Satan focuses on this area is that these powers are so sacred. The power of procreation is what contributes to God's greatness. Only he has the power to give life. Without God, life cannot be created or sustained. Part of what it means to be like God is to have that power; hence, the power that can make us most like God is the power Satan targets. The power to procreate is so sacred that it cannot be misused without dire consequences. Proper use of these powers is the closest thing to godhood any mortal can experience on earth. That's why the Lord has commanded us to marry (see Genesis 2:24), and the reason why he created the earth (see D&C 49:15–16), so we can be parents on earth in preparation for heavenly parenthood. You'll note the three most grievous sins listed by the Lord in Alma 39:3–6 all deal with abuses of the powers of life. Denying the Holy Ghost results in spiritual death. Murder causes physical death. Immorality is a violation of the power to beget life.

Paul gives us the key to protecting our virtue. He says to have your loins "girt about with truth." How is that accomplished? Truth is found in the scriptures. Truth, light, and Spirit are all connected. Girding oneself with truth is filling one's mind, heart, and life with light and the influence of the Holy Ghost. "For the word of the Lord is truth, and whatsoever is truth is light, and whatsoever is light is Spirit, even the Spirit of Jesus Christ" (D&C 84:45).

Constant scripture study, both with the family and individually, will help accomplish this. Daily reading in the Book of Mormon in particular provides us with needed spiritual nourishment. Nephi put it this way: "Wherefore, I said unto you, feast upon the words of Christ; for behold, the words of Christ will tell you all things what ye should do" (2 Nephi 32:3). If you haven't already developed a daily habit of scripture study, commit yourself to do so. If you already have such a habit, strengthen your armor by making your scripture study more earnest and purposeful.

President Benson suggests thirty minutes per day of reading in the Book of Mormon (see *A Witness and a Warning* [Salt Lake City: Deseret Book, 1988], p. 8). Make a commitment today that you'll never remove this symbolic armor from your loins. Commit yourself to a specific amount of scripture study daily.

HEART

Our next area of concern is the heart, symbolizing our conduct. How does one go about receiving a change of heart? Can a heart be changed? Some psychologists suggest that our nature cannot be changed. A prophet of God has a differing point of view: "Can human hearts be changed? Why, of course! It happens every day in the great missionary work of the Church. It is one of the most widespread of Christ's modern miracles. If it hasn't happened to you—it should. . . . The Lord works from the inside out. The world works from the outside. The world would take people out of the slums. Christ takes the slums out of people, and then they take themselves out of the slums. The world would mold men by changing their environment. Christ changes men, who then change their environment. The world would shape human behavior, but Christ can change human nature" (Ezra Taft Benson, *A Witness and a Warning*, pp. 62–64).

Once again, the key to our protection is found in the scriptures. On a mission to reclaim apostate Zoramites, Alma offered this amazing insight: "And now, as the preaching of the word had a great tendency to lead the people to do that which was just—yea, it had had more powerful effect upon the minds of the people than the sword, or anything else, which happened unto them— therefore Alma thought it was expedient that they should try the virtue of the word of God" (Alma 31:5).

The word of God is more powerful than anything else! Can the word of God truly change one's heart? Elder Boyd K. Packer has taught us that it can. "True doctrine, understood, changes attitudes and behavior. The study of the doctrines of the gospel will improve behavior quicker than a study of behavior will improve behavior. . . . That is why we stress so forcefully the study of the doctrines of the gospel" (*Ensign*, November 1986, p. 17).

Measuring a change of heart is a difficult task. It's not like measuring progress in a weight lifting class or a history class, where improvement in performance is easily graded. Although the task was difficult, I attempted to measure the changes in hearts caused by the power of the word while teaching seminary in Mesa, Arizona. On the second day of class, I gave the students a blank sheet of paper. I asked them to write their feelings about God, Christ, the Church, and Joseph Smith. I told them I would not look at what they had written, so they could be completely honest. The papers were folded over, stapled, and the student's name and the date were written on the outside. I filed them away until the end of the school year. We studied doctrine for nine months. We marked and annotated more than 1,200 verses of scripture that year. We let the power of the word work on our minds and hearts. Then, during the last week of school, I repeated the procedure. Only after they were done recording their feelings the second time did I return their first paper to them, so they could compare the two testimonies. Although I had told the students I would never see what they wrote, some students elected to share with me what they had written. Following are two excerpts from my "before" and "after" experiment with the power of the word.

The first was by a girl named Julie. Her first response read:

"I guess I sometimes wonder if Christ really does live. I don't know for sure. . . . I do wonder if this is the true church or not. Everything we are told to do seems right, but I still have doubts."

Notice the difference in her later response:

"This year I have really grown. . . . I know that God lives and that his son Jesus Christ is my brother and really knows me and cares for me. I know that He has a body of flesh and bones. . . . Through prayer I know that He will guide us and show us the right way through His prophets, which I know were really called of God.

"The Church of Jesus Christ of Latter-day Saints is the only true church, and I know without a doubt that it was restored by Joseph Smith, who was a true prophet."

A second example comes from a boy named Larry. His first response:

"I don't really know that there is a God. I only go to Church to make my dad and mom happy.

"I wish I had a testimony but I don't. Sometimes I feel like I have an important job on earth but I don't know what it is. I am always wanting to do something wrong."

Now his second response:

"I know that the Church is true. I have a testimony of the Church. I love my Big Brother, my Heavenly Father, and know that they live.

"I know that Joseph Smith was and is the first president of our Father's church on earth. I have a testimony. . . . I love this church with all my life. Some say they do not know if they would give their life for it, but I know that if need be, and if my Father willed it, I would."

These are only two examples of the "power of the word." President Ezra Taft Benson has promised: "When individual members and families immerse themselves in the scriptures regularly and consistently, other areas of activity will automatically come. Testimonies will increase. Commitment will be strengthened. Families will be fortified. Personal revelation will flow" (*Ensign*, May 1986, p. 79).

The power of the word to change one's heart should not be underestimated. Conversely, failure to study the scriptures daily removes a critical portion of the armor and leaves our heart exposed to the world, its temptations, and its set of values.

FEET

Our feet represent our goals in life. Someone once said, "Show me a man's friends and I will show you the man." Our choice of friends in large part determines the path our feet will take. In the Gospel of Mark, the Savior gave very strong counsel concerning the types of friends who would lead us away from the path of righteousness: "If thy brother offend thee and confess not and forsake not, he shall be cut off. . . . For it is better for thee to enter into life without thy brother, than for thee and thy brother to be cast into hell; . . . Therefore, let every man stand or fall, by himself, and not for another; or not trusting another. . . . For it is better that thyself should be saved, than to be cast into hell with thy brother" (JST Mark 9:40–48).

The Savior counsels us to "cut off" friends who would stray from the straight path and take us with them. Choosing correct goals is important. Choosing the type of friends who will allow and help us to reach those goals is equally important.

HEAD

President Harold B. Lee suggested that the head in Paul's analogy of the armor symbolizes one's thinking. Our thinking is largely shaped by the world around us. Elder Boyd K. Packer expressed his concern in general conference about the influence of the world on the youth. He gave this caution concerning the dress, conduct, and music of the world and its influence on the thinking of the youth: "For the past several years we have watched patterns of reverence and irreverence in the Church. While many are to be highly commended, we are drifting. We have reason to be deeply concerned. The world grows increasingly noisy. Clothing and grooming and conduct are looser and sloppier and more disheveled. Raucous music with obscene lyrics blasted through amplifiers . . . characterizes the drug culture. Variations of these things are gaining wide acceptance and influence over our youth. . . . This trend to more noise, more excitement, more contention, less restraint, less dignity, less formality is not coincidental nor innocent nor harmless. The first order issued by a commander mounting a military invasion is the jamming of the channels of communication of those he intends to conquer. Irreverence suits the purposes of the adversary by obstructing the delicate channels of revelation in both mind and spirit" (*Ensign*, November 1991, p. 22). Allowing the influences of the world to shape our thinking impairs revelation, the channel the Lord has provided to communicate with us.

Elder Packer also spoke in conference about the shield of faith. Note what he says about how it is made, who polishes it, who fits it on, and what causes the shield of faith to be removed from one's armor. Elder Packer stated: "Our Father's plan requires that, like the generation of life itself, the shield of faith is to be made and fitted in the family. . . .

"The plan designed by the Father contemplates that man and woman, husband and wife, working together, fit each child individually with a shield of faith made to buckle on so firmly that it can neither be pulled off nor penetrated by those fiery darts.

"It takes the steady strength of a father to hammer out the metal of it and the tender hands of a mother to polish and fit it on. Sometimes one parent is left to do it alone. It is difficult, but it can be done.

"In the Church we can teach about the materials from which a shield of faith is made: reverence, courage, chastity, repentance, forgiveness, compassion. . . . But the actual making of and fitting on of the shield of faith belongs in the family circle. Otherwise it may loosen and come off in a crisis. . . .

"Our leaders press members to understand that what is most worth doing must be done at home. Some still do not see that too many out-of-home activities, however well intended, leave too little time to make and fit on the shield of faith at home" (*Ensign*, May 1995, pp. 8–9).

The youth of the Church cannot view lightly the role of their parents and family in keeping their armor snugly in place. It's a temptation to replace family time and home activities with other interests. Being involved in too many out-of-home activities dangerously sets the shield of faith aside, leaving us subject to the fiery darts of the wicked.

In summary, Paul counsels us to put on the whole armor of God for protection against the fiery darts of the adversary. We have four major areas that need protecting. Our loins symbolize our virtue. The truth we receive from studying the scriptures protects this virtue. Our heart represents our conduct. Our heart also is deeply affected by our study of the doctrines of the gospel. Our feet symbolize our goals. The choice of proper friends will directly influence setting and achieving proper goals. Our head represents our thinking. We must avoid certain influences of the world to keep the delicate channel of revelation open to influence our thinking.

In an earlier letter to the Romans, Paul refers to this armor as the "armour of light" (Romans 13:12). That seems fitting since most of the protective power of the armor is based on light received from the word of God found in the scriptures. This word affects our virtue, our hearts, our goals, and our minds.

It's my prayer that none of us will put ourselves at risk by failing to put on the armor of light or by later removing it once it is in place. We all need the whole armor of God so that we will be able to stand.

Todd B. Parker set a state record in the pole vault in high school. He holds a bachelor's degree from Weber State University and M.Ed. and Ed.D. degrees from Brigham Young University. He has taught seminary and institute and has participated in EFY every year since its beginning in 1976.

22

FUN OR HAPPINESS

Kim M. Peterson

Fun is a strange concept. Don't get me wrong—I love fun. But have you ever noticed that we don't "do" fun, we "have" fun. It's hard even to define fun. What is fun to you may be boring to others. Linguistically, you can't *be* fun, but your friends can claim that you are or are not fun. Some people don't even know when they're having fun. It's true. Haven't you heard someone ask, "Are we having fun yet?" Fun is a strange concept.

So where do you have the most fun? Where would you be and what would you be doing if you wanted to have fun? When did that become fun to you? Once you identify a place and an activity, see if you can do with your activity what I can do with mine.

I remember vividly when for me the idea of helicopter skiing became fun. One dismal February day when I was in the eighth grade, our boys gym class piled into the wrestling room, sat down in teams, answered the roll call, and listened intently to our coach. He informed us that because we had been working so hard, he wanted to reward us with a movie. Sure enough, in the back of the room there was a 16mm projector. The coach turned off the lights and started the film.

Sitting cross-legged on the vinyl mat, I watched an amazing panorama unfold before my eyes: the Bugaboo mountain range of Western Canada. Suddenly, two skiers broke the uncut snow and descended the mountain, making "figure eights" in the bottomless powder. From that moment, the "funnest" experience I could imagine was to be skiing in the Bugaboos.

Even thinking about going skiing in the Bugaboos would make my stomach jump. If I thought I was going to be able to ski the Bugaboos, training, saving money, and cleaning my room to find lost ski equipment would all be enjoyable. Buying an airplane ticket, packing my bags, and boarding the plane would all add to my excitement, if I was anticipating skiing the Bugaboos.

Landing in Canada, finding a room, trying to sleep, and waking up the next morning would be part of the fun. But the adrenaline would really begin to pump at the point where I would load my skis into the helicopter, strap in, and take off. It's hard to imagine how much fun it would be to exit the helicopter, tighten my boots, and click into my bindings. Twenty-one years of built-up anticipation would hardly allow me to be calm were I able to grasp my poles, push off a Bugaboo ridge, and dive into deep, uncut powder! At that moment, however, the amount of fun would begin shrinking.

The nature of fun is such that after my first turn, the fun would begin to diminish. Don't misunderstand, making turns in powder is certainly more fun for me than cleaning the garage, doing the dishes, or folding clothes. But the first five turns are, in some ways, more fun than the next five turns. In fact, as my thighs would begin to burn and as I would begin to breathe a little heavier, the fun would continue to diminish. By the time I finished my run, the fun would have taken a significant dive.

I expect that the next flight up the mountain would be a little less exciting than the first, and that each successive trip would be less and less fun. The anticipation of fun is almost more fun than the fun itself. Repacking, boarding the plane, landing, claiming my baggage, and driving home from the airport would be considerably less fun. By the next day I would be at the bottom of the fun meter . . . worse than if I had never gone to the Bugaboos.

The truth is that fun always ends, and after the fun is over it's often worse than if we had never had fun in the first place.

After the children of Israel had witnessed the plagues visited on their Egyptian tormentors, and after God had delivered the Israelites from Pharaoh by parting the Red Sea, Moses ascended the mountain of the Lord. While on the mountain, Moses was given two tablets of testimony "written with the finger of God" (Exodus 31:18). Can you imagine how precious those tablets would be? They contained God's handwriting.

While Moses was on the mountain, the children of Israel became distracted. Because they didn't know what had become of Moses, they fashioned their own gods. The next day they ate and "rose up to play" (Exodus 32:6). Apparently, worshipping the golden calf was more fun than waiting for the Lord. God told Moses to get down off the mountain, "for thy people, which thou broughtest out of the land of Egypt, have corrupted themselves: they have turned aside quickly" (Exodus 32:7–8).

As modern-day children of Israel, many of us fashion our own gods because they are more fun. For some, the pursuit of pleasure is only temporarily interrupted by moments of worship. Like Moses' wayward followers, we corrupt ourselves with fun and turn aside quickly from obeying the things we know are right.

Maybe you know some youth who think drinking alcohol is more fun than obeying the Word of Wisdom, but who never seem satisfied after they drink. Maybe you have heard of some who thought that engaging in immoral sexual activities was more fun than living a chaste life, but who were obviously miserable after a few moments of supposed pleasure. Maybe you know some who thought cheating was more fun than doing honest work, but who were disappointed by their unearned grades. Satan has told us two lies: (1) committing sin is all right and (2) sinning is fun. Like a first-time smoker who has to convince his or her body to like tobacco, sinners must convince themselves that sin is fun. First-time sinners are frequently disappointed to discover that sinning wasn't even that much fun. To Alma's declaration that "wickedness never was happiness" (Alma 41:10) we must add that wickedness usually isn't even fun!

Happiness is an entirely different thing. On my first visit to a health club, I tried to figure out how to use some of the weight machines. After I had tried unsuccessfully to bench-press 125 pounds, one of the trainers asked me if I needed some help. I think it was a nice way of saying that I was obviously unfamiliar with how to use the machines. Patiently, he took me to each machine and recorded on his clipboard the meager weight I could comfortably lift. After I had completed a "circuit" (one time on each machine), the training began.

My trainer asked if it was my goal to get stronger. I must have looked pretty weak next to him. One of his thighs was as big as both of mine. His arms and chest were huge! I told him I did want to get stronger, so he started what he called a "negative workout." At each station he had me lift the most weight I could lift by myself, just one time. Then he helped me get the weight up several more times, until I was unable to budge it at all. We repeated the process at each station. When we finished the workout, I was physically exhausted.

My trainer told me to come back in three days and left. I shuffled into the locker room, aching for a shower. Standing in front of my locker, I discovered that I was too weak even to lift the handle of my locker! I was weaker than when I had started. I managed to open the locker only by holding the handle with my fingers and using my leg muscles to push my hand up.

The next challenge was to lift my arms high enough to turn on the shower. Only by rocking my body back and forth could I swing my arms high enough to reach the faucet. I must have stood under the shower for a half hour, too weak to move. Laboriously, I toweled off and got dressed. Then I dragged myself to my car, swung my arms to reach the door handle, and painfully climbed into the driver's seat. All I can remember about that night is collapsing into bed.

Morning found me lying spread-eagled; it felt as though rigor mortis had set in. I was quite sure that I wasn't going to be able to move a single joint or limb of my body. A hot shower helped a little. That day I barely had the strength to lift a fork, write my name, or carry a backpack. Two days later I was back at the gym. The trainer laughed knowingly when I told him about my inability to lift a pencil, and then we began the workout routine again. As I worked, my muscles warmed up, and the pain diminished. Subsequent workouts were less difficult, and I discovered that the longer I persisted, the stronger I got. The more I worked, the more my muscles responded.

A state of happiness can be reached only by following a similar process of work and reward. When we first endeavor to find happiness, we are seemingly unrewarded. For example, very few people have a completely satisfying experience the first time they attempt to read the scriptures. Frequently, people tell me the scriptures are boring and hard to understand. As in the negative workout, the happiness that is available through an understanding of the scriptures seems to come only after making an initial investment of time and effort—after making a sacrifice.

One of the great descriptions of happiness in the Book of

Mormon is found in Lehi's vision of the Tree of Life. If the
field (1 Nephi 8:9) is a symbol of the world and the fruit of
the tree (1 Nephi 8:10) is a symbol of eternal life, then the
journey to get to the tree must represent the choices we
make in this life.

After Lehi tasted the fruit of the tree, he said that it was
desirable and that it filled his soul "with exceedingly great
joy" (1 Nephi 8:12). What a marvelous description of the
pursuit of eternal life. Striving, working, trying, and waiting for eternal life will bring us exceedingly great joy in the
end. In order to get to the tree, however, we must "cling"
to the iron rod (1 Nephi 8:24). Persistence in reading the
scriptures may not seem fun, but it ultimately will result in
exceedingly great joy. By clinging to the iron rod and listening to their father, Nephi and Sam experienced great joy
in partaking of the fruit of the Tree of Life. Laman and
Lemuel would not partake of the fruit. Reading the
accounts of their experiences, I've never gotten the impression that Nephi's rebellious brothers were particularly
happy men.

In Nephi and Laman we have examples of what a difference attitude can make and of the differences between
fun and happiness. Both Nephi and Laman left Jerusalem.
Both Nephi and Laman returned to Jerusalem for the brass
plates. Both Nephi and Laman returned to Jerusalem for
Ishmael and his family. Both Nephi and Laman participated in building the ship. Both Nephi and Laman
boarded the ship. Both Nephi and Laman landed in the
Promised Land. What was the difference between Nephi
and Laman? One profound difference is that Nephi saw
each of these challenges as necessary and approached each
task willingly. Laman murmured.

In our pursuit of happiness, whom do we resemble
most? Are we more like Nephi or like Laman? Do you go
willingly to church or murmur and go to church? Do you
honor your parents or murmur and obey your parents? Do

you eagerly read your scriptures or murmur and read your scriptures? Will you wait patiently until you are sixteen to date or will you murmur and wait to date until you are sixteen? I'm convinced that murmuring keeps us from experiencing both fun and happiness.

In their journey from Jerusalem to the Promised Land, Lehi and his family provided us with a symbol of our journey from this life to eternal life with Heavenly Father. Their difficult experience contains many parallels to our attempt to successfully negotiate mortality.

After the family had traveled 250 miles into the wilderness, Lehi asked his sons to go all the way back to Jerusalem to obtain the brass plates. Nephi went and did as the Lord commanded (see 1 Nephi 3:7); Laman murmured and went and did as the Lord commanded (see 1 Nephi 3:5). The scriptures are frequently linked with joy. When Nephi and Laman returned with the scriptures, Lehi and Sariah did "rejoice exceedingly" (1 Nephi 5:9). Likewise, we ought to rejoice exceedingly that we have scriptures to guide us in our effort to return to Heavenly Father.

After walking 500 miles, both Nephi and Laman walked 500 more to bring Ishmael's family into the wilderness with them. In our journey back to Heavenly Father, we are not expected to go alone. Marriage is ordained of God, so that we may each have a companion in our quest. After noting that he and his brothers each married one of the daughters of Ishmael, Nephi described himself as having "been blessed of the Lord exceedingly" (1 Nephi 16:8). Our families are a source of profound happiness.

In the same chapter, Lehi discovered the ball of curious workmanship, and the family learned that the Liahona only worked in response to faith and diligence. Similarly, the gift of the Holy Ghost is given to every member of the Church. If we pay attention to its promptings, strive diligently, and follow by faith, the Holy Ghost will lead us to happiness.

The next challenge to Lehi's family came in the form of Nephi's broken bow. Lost in the wilderness with no means of obtaining food, Nephi didn't give up. Instead, he made a bow and an arrow, asked his father to seek direction from the Liahona, and proceeded to hunt for food. I frequently let small inconveniences keep me from being happy. Not having a car, not being asked to a dance, or not making the team—these are not reasons to be unhappy. Overcoming trials can also result in great happiness. When Nephi returned with food, his family had "great joy" (1 Nephi 16:32).

When they reached the land Bountiful, it appeared as though Lehi's family could be happy at last. There, Nephi was instructed to build a ship. Laman and Lemuel were at first skeptical that it could be done, and they mocked their younger brother, then threatened to drown him. Nephi rebuked them for their lack of faith and exercised "the power of God" to convince them to help in the construction. Perhaps Lehi's band was never more vulnerable than when they were in the middle of the ocean, on a ship built by their own hands, and guided by a ball of curious workmanship. Foolishly, Laman and Lemuel forgot to heed the Lord and commenced to "make themselves merry" (1 Nephi 18:9). Sometimes we risk losing happiness in a quest for fun, when we need most to depend on the Lord.

When Nephi tried to warn his brothers, Laman and Lemuel bound his hands. Even though the ball quit working and the winds became contrary, they wouldn't let Nephi go. Finally, to avoid certain destruction, they loosed Nephi's bands. He took the ball in his swollen hands, and it immediately began to work again. Because of his faith and diligence, Nephi was able to lead his family to the Promised Land.

The desire to have fun often interferes with following

the prophet. Young men who can't separate themselves from having fun to serve missions miss an opportunity to find real happiness in serving the Lord. In Doctrine and Covenants 18:15, the Lord describes the "great joy" that results from bringing even one soul to Him. When Nephi finally succeeded in separating his family from his brothers' families, he and his people enjoyed a time of peace when they were not hindered by rebellious attitudes. They were able to live the gospel. Of their experience, Nephi recorded, "And it came to pass that we lived after the manner of happiness" (2 Nephi 5:27).

Fun and happiness are not mutually exclusive. Certainly we can be happy while having fun, but having fun is not the extent of happiness. The hope we have is that we will one day be able to replace temporary gratification with eternal happiness. Like Lehi and Nephi, I know that following the scriptures, living together in families, obeying the Holy Ghost, overcoming trials, and following wise counsel are the things that make it possible to live after the manner of happiness.

Kim M. Peterson is a seminary and institute instructor in the Denver, Colorado, area. He loves to ski and has been employed in the wintertime as a ski instructor. He also enjoys cooking a variety of "eastern dishes." Kim and his wife, Terri, have two children. He has a goal never to become an "R.M." (Ask him what he means by that when you get a chance.)

$$23$$

GET OFF THE BENCH!

Matt Richardson

A few years ago, my son wanted a football uniform for Christmas. I'm sure that you know the type: a plastic helmet bearing your favorite team's insignia, an "official" jersey, miniature shoulder pads, and a pair of nylon pants that are either way too short or four sizes too large. (Zach's were too large!) On Christmas morning, Zachary found his package under the tree and frantically clawed the paper away to reveal his coveted football uniform. I still remember the jubilant smile he wore while pumping his arm in the air and saying, "Yes! Santa loves me!" My wife and I smiled and winked at each other. Zach didn't waste any time putting that uniform on. As soon as it was on, he charged throughout the house "scoring touchdowns" and "blocking" his little sister. (We later had to make that a penalty—illegal block to the sister.) I remember hearing a little growl, like an engine running, and I would look down to find Zachary clinging to my leg. "What are you doing?" I would ask. "I'm tackling you, Dad!"

Zachary loved his little uniform. He wore it all day long. When it came time to eat dinner, Zachary sat at the table with his helmet strapped securely to his head. We asked him to take it off, but he quickly informed us that "real football players eat with their helmets on." Since it was Christmas, we thought it wouldn't hurt to let him try. Besides, it was funny watching him try to guide the spoon through the face mask to his mouth. Zachary slept in that football uniform, because, after all, "real football players sleep in their uniforms." Needless to say, Zachary wore that uniform for days. I was worried that maybe he was "too much into the uniform thing." My wife chuckled and said that she thought I was probably just like that when I was a kid. Although I denied it, she was absolutely right. I couldn't wait to get a uniform when I was Zach's age.

I remember as a kid looking through my older brother's high school yearbook and finding the sports section. I longingly looked at the teams in their uniforms and yearned to be part of them. As I flipped through the pages, I came across a section that had "Mighty Men, Model Men, Murray [the name of my high school] Men" written in bold letters across the top. That sounded so cool, I had to read it again. "Mighty Men, Model Men, Murray Men." Below this title were pictures of young men all wearing the same type of jacket. I recognized some of them from the team pictures on the previous pages, but not everyone in the team picture was in this "Mighty Man" section . . . only some. I learned later that this was the "Letterman's Club" picture. Right then and there, I decided that I wanted to be a letterman. I didn't have the slightest idea what a letterman was, but I wanted to be one.

I later found out that the letterperson designation wasn't exclusive to sports but included members of clubs, the choir, student government, academics, and other groups. When it came to letterpersons, however, it wasn't enough to simply be part of the organization, wear their uniform, or go to their meetings. According to standards at my high school, a letterperson had to "make a significant contribution to the success of the organization." In other words, a letterperson was a necessary part of the organization—one that the organization couldn't do without.

With today's challenges, we have need of more letterpersons in life. That's right, life! As a matter of fact, even our prophets have talked about life in terms of a game. President Ezra Taft Benson once said: "You are a royal generation. The heavenly grandstands are cheering you on. The Lord is our coach and manager. His team will win and we can be a valiant part of it if we so desire. Rise up, O youth of Zion! You hardly realize the great divine potential that lies within you" ("In His Steps," in *Speeches of the Year,* 1979 [Provo: Brigham Young University Press, 1980], p. 59).

Just think: you are part of that unique team—the team of Jesus Christ. You joined his team when you were baptized, and you put on his uniform as you "took his name upon you." It has been written that "your generation will fight the greatest army of Satanic hosts ever assembled" (*Church News,* May 9, 1991). As we face such stern opposition, we will need every member of the team to "make a significant contribution." We don't just need more members, we need more letterpersons for Christ. Therefore, how are you treating your uniform of Christ? You are wearing it, aren't you?

John the Beloved had a warning for those who would wear Christ's uniform in the latter days. Speaking through John, the Lord said, "I know thy works, that thou art neither cold nor hot: I would thou wert cold or hot. So then because thou art lukewarm, and neither cold nor hot, I will spue thee out of my mouth" (Revelation 3:15–16). John is pleading with us to stand up, make a difference, be identified with the uniform of Christ that we are wearing. We live in a time when we can't sit on the back row, halfheartedly living the gospel standards. We need to turn up the temperature, make our contribution. So how does someone become a letterperson for Jesus Christ? How do we make a significant contribution to the success of the

Church and the gospel of Christ? May I suggest three ideas for your consideration.

STAND UP FOR YOUR TEAM!

Something special happens when we learn to stand up for . . . almost anything. Power comes from loyalty and devotion. For example, I remember playing tennis with two of my older brothers and my older sister at a park near my home. Playing tennis on the court next to ours were two boys, the same age as my sister. While they were playing, they said something about my sister that was rude. My sister, a very sensitive person, heard what they said and started to cry. I was trying to comfort her when I heard a loud clang. It came from the gate between the two tennis courts as it banged shut after my brothers ran through it. You see, these boys made the comment loudly enough that not just my sister but my older brothers heard it as well. By the time I raced through the gate and onto the other court, my older brothers had already captured their prey. One of my brothers was sitting on the chest of one young man, and my other brother had his prey pinned against the fence. I remember my brothers saying, "Nobody says anything like that about my sister . . . nobody!" I must confess I was confused because I was thinking to myself, "Wait a minute, you said that very thing to her just last night!" But something important was happening. When push came to shove, I learned that as brothers and sisters, we stood up for each other. If you are going to fight one Richardson, you will have to fight us all.

It is one thing to stand up for your family, but it is equally important to stand up for the gospel. In actuality it isn't that much different, and it can happen in a variety of ways. I used to ride the bus to school. I remember arriving at the bus stop one day and finding the other students huddled together in a group. As I approached, one of my friends popped his head up out of the huddle, and he shouted anxiously at me to "hurry up." As I got closer, other friends began yelling to me, "Come on, Matt. Hurry up." Then I heard them saying, "You just wait. Matt will show you—you just wait!"

"Hi, guys!" I said cheerily, sensing that something was up.

"Show him, Matt. You just tell him!"

"Tell who . . . what?" I asked. There in the middle of the group was Ronnie, the neighborhood anti-Mormon. He had told my friends that Mormon kids were nothing more than a bunch of sheep. That we didn't know the first thing about our church and that we just followed our parents around, doing whatever they said. Bless my friends' hearts, they had stood up to Ronnie. "No, we're not," they had said confidently, "we're not sheep!"

"Prove it," Ronnie shot back. "Tell me one thing about your church."

My friends were really confident now. "Okay, Ronnie," they said, "you just wait till Matt Richardson gets here; he'll tell you all about our church." There I stood— shocked.

"Come on, Mormon," Ronnie smirked, "one thing."

My mind went blank. The only thing I could think of about the Church was refreshments and church basketball, and neither one of those seemed to be what was needed. Luckily, the bus came and we got on. "Saved by the bus!" I thought.

Ronnie didn't let up, however. "Come on, Mormon, one thing," he repeated, and then he started making sheep calls. I was so frustrated. I remember saying a *real* prayer in my heart. Ronnie was relentless. And then it hit me. I sat up straight and looked Ronnie square in the eyes. "Ronnie," I started. "We believe in God the Eternal Father, and in His Son, Jesus Christ, and in the Holy Ghost." I just kept on going. "We believe that men will be punished for their own sins . . ." I didn't stop until I had recited all thirteen Articles of Faith. There was a purpose for Primary after all!

I wish that I could tell you that we stopped by the local swimming pool on the way to school to baptize Ronnie, but it didn't happen that way. As a matter of fact, I don't know what ever happened to Ronnie. He moved from our neighborhood shortly after that experience, and I haven't seen or heard from him since. Although Ronnie didn't get off the bus a different person, there was somebody who did—me! I knew that what I had told Ronnie was true. I realized that I knew more about the gospel of Jesus Christ than I thought I did and, even more important, I had stood up for my team.

Maybe this is what Paul meant as he boldly declared that he was ready to teach the gospel, even in Rome (where his life would be taken). He was a prime example of one who stood up for Christ's gospel, for Paul was "not ashamed of the gospel of Christ" (Romans 1:16). This same attitude was reflected in the early Apostles who were commanded by the Sanhedrin council "not to speak at all nor teach in the name of Jesus" (Acts 4:18). But the Apostles were always found teaching thereafter in the name of Christ. The council arrested them again and threatened them, scolded them, and on occasion even beat them. "Did not we straitly command you that ye should not teach in [Jesus'] name?" a frustrated and wicked council member inquired of the Apostles (Acts 5:28). Undaunted, Peter and the other Apostles answered, "We ought to obey God rather than men" (Acts 5:29). Stand up, O youth of Zion!

KEEP YOUR UNIFORM ON AT ALL TIMES

One of the keys to the success of any team or organization is to always know who is on your side. You can imagine how disastrous it would be if someone from the opposing team posed as a fellow team member, or if one of your team members decided to change to the opposing team in the middle of the game. Think how confusing and frustrating it would be if you had some members of either team wearing half of your uniform and half of the other team's uniform. In a way, a uniform tells you who you can trust and who you can't.

In order to make a significant contribution to Christ's team, his players must keep their uniforms on at all times. Christ's players cannot afford to take off any part of his uniform, even for just a moment. Perhaps this is what Alma was emphasizing when he admonished us to "stand as witnesses of God at all times and in all things, and in all places that ye may be in" (Mosiah 18:9). In a way, that is exactly what we promise each time we partake of the sacrament. To those members who faithfully wear the uniform of Christ at all times, in all things, in every place, and under all circumstances, come significant understanding, comfort, and blessings. Paul wrote to a group of Saints who were struggling with this very problem (standing up for the gospel) and encouraged them to "be zealously affected always in a good thing, and not only when I am present with you" (Galatians 4:18). A good question may be, How does becoming a letterperson for Christ relate to Paul's invitation to "be zealously affected"? Perhaps this example will help answer that question.

During my senior year in high school, my car would run out of gas on a regular basis. On one occasion, I remember putting gasoline in my car only to find that it still wouldn't start. My best friend and I quickly discovered that my fuel line was blocked and that gasoline wasn't getting to the engine. I remembered my father once telling me an experience from his younger days, when he had had a similar problem. He filled a soda pop bottle with gasoline and poured the gasoline straight into the carburetor, thus bypassing the fuel line altogether. I relayed this story to my best friend, and we decided to try my dad's old trick. We filled a large paint can with gas and walked from the gas station back to my car. By the time we arrived, it was dark and the street was only dimly lit by a single street lamp on the corner. We raised the hood and uncovered the carburetor, and then I jumped into the driver's seat. With the hood raised, my vision of what was happening was obstructed except through a small space between the raised hood and the bottom of the windshield. I could barely see Kurt's hands and part of the gasoline-filled paint can through the small gap. I watched as Kurt carefully tipped the can and poured gasoline into the carburetor. "Hit it!" Kurt yelled. I quickly turned the key and heard the whirling grind, but the car still didn't start. As soon as I turned the key off, I could see Kurt pour more gas into the open carburetor. "Try it again!" he yelled. I turned the key and pumped the gas pedal with the same results— nothing. "I don't think this will work," I yelled to Kurt. "Third time's a charm," Kurt hollered back as he poured some more gas into the carburetor. "Try it again!" I turned the key but, unlike the times before, the engine cranked over only once. Then there was a loud bang, and a bright flash of light darted through the hood's gap where I was watching. I couldn't remember anything about bangs and flashes from my dad's story. What followed next was something that I will never forget. I looked out of the passenger window and saw my best friend engulfed in flames from his knees to his head. He literally lit up the dark night as he whirled around in circles, frantically slapping at the flames. I remember how everything happened so fast . . . but at the same time so slow. I realized that I was screaming in my mind: *Stop! Drop! Roll!* But Kurt wasn't stopping, he wasn't dropping, and he definitely wasn't rolling!

The next thing I remember was sitting on Kurt's chest, slapping his head with my hands, trying to put the flames out. I had gotten out of the car, chased him down, tackled him, and now I was so scared that I was trying hard not to cry as I was extinguishing the flames. I suddenly realized that Kurt was no longer on fire, but I was still slapping him. I also realized that now I was really screaming at him. "Why didn't you stop, drop, and roll?" Kurt was trying to answer, which is actually quite difficult to do with someone sitting on your chest and slapping your face and head like a deranged madman. "I was trying to," Kurt would say between slaps. After I came to my senses and realized that Kurt was no longer on fire, I hurried to take care of my car, which was also burning. As soon as everything was under control, I returned to Kurt and asked, "Why didn't you stop, drop, and roll?" He simply replied that he had wanted to save his baseball jacket.

I have thought about that experience many times over the intervening years. I hope we would never put our lives at risk over any thing, but I have thought about the power of Kurt's determination to save his jacket in light of Paul's admonition to the Saints in Galatia regarding being "zealously affected." Just think if we, as members of Christ's team, were empowered with Kurt's zeal to save and keep the uniform of Christ on at all times. With such determination, we wouldn't remove the uniform of Christ, even at the peril of our own life. This reminds me of Paul, as he taught the Saints in his letter to the Ephesians to "take unto you the whole armour of God, that ye may be able to withstand in the evil day, having done all, to stand" (Ephesians 6:13). Do we really think that we can go into the battles of life having left part of our armor at home and still escape unscathed? Can we take off part of our armor during a party, on a date, while watching certain videos, or in almost anything we do without the opposition exploiting our weakness? Don't you think that the enemy would easily recognize a missing piece of an opponent's armor? Do you honestly believe that if a soldier was found without his breastplate during a battle, the enemy would incessantly pound away on his helmet (or some other protected area) and not strike at the exposed chest? Not likely. We must follow Paul's advice to wear *all* of the uniform of Christ's team—at all times.

WEAR YOUR UNIFORM WITH HONOR AND DIGNITY

Finally, we realize there is a great, even unique, strength that is enjoyed by members of a team who represent their team or organization with honor and dignity. I used to treat my sports uniforms with special care. I guess they were special because they were more than fabric. They represented my city, my school, my classmates, and my fellow teammates. I remember watching my wife as a bride, dressed in her wedding dress, walk with great care so as not to soil her dress. But even more impressive than her dress was the way she walked. She glowed with confidence, happiness, and a bright vision of her future. Her uniform (dress) surely made her feel beautiful, but at the same time and even more significantly, she brought beauty to her dress.

In a similar yet far more meaningful way, I think of a pair of gloves my wife has that she treats with great respect. I remember the first time that she showed me her gloves. She took them out carefully and displayed them with great pride. By the way she was behaving, I figured that these gloves must be made of silk or that they were antiques—something had to be special about these gloves, judging by the way she treated them. To my surprise they were simple, white cotton gloves, not really that *special* at all. But then my wife told me their history. "The last time I wore these gloves, I was eight years old. These are the gloves that I wore when I shook the hand of President Spencer W. Kimball, the prophet of God!" I suddenly realized why they were so important. My wife's reverence for what they represented made them important. They reminded her of the deep love she had for a prophet of God.

My wife's gloves remind me of a similar experience

concerning the uniform of Christ. While standing in line to eat dinner as missionaries in the MTC, my companion and I decided to go to the foyer, where pictures of all the apostles hung, and see if we could name them all by sight. As we were standing in front of their portraits trying to put names with faces, I heard a small, tender voice behind me. Although it was not directed at me, I knew that it was *about* me. I turned around to see a small girl holding hands with her grandmother. "Grandma," she asked, "are those *real* missionaries?" Her little finger was outstretched and pointed directly at me. "Yes, honey," her grandma answered, "those are *real* missionaries!" To fully understand this experience, you must understand that this little girl didn't simply ask if we were missionaries, she asked if we were *real* missionaries, and the way she asked it made it sound like she was asking her grandma about celebrities or somebody really special. I remember bending over to shake her hand and introduce myself. "My name is Elder Richardson and this is my companion. We have been called to teach the gospel of Christ in Denmark." Then I had to say it. "And yes, we are *real* missionaries!" I felt so special, so empowered, so proud of being a missionary, it was hard to resist singing "High on the Mountain Top" at the top of my lungs.

I will never forget that little girl. She looked at me with such wonder that it made me feel honorable and special. She looked at the uniform of a missionary, complete with the black name tag, as something that was so important, it made me feel important. It was just like my wife's gloves. They were important and special because they were treated in a special way. I felt special as a missionary, at that time, because a small girl treated me like I was special.

I thought often about that experience throughout my mission. Whenever I felt that I was in a compromising situation, the memory of that little girl would come to mind, particularly her little voice: "Grandma, are those *real* missionaries?" I wondered what that little girl would think if she saw me making a wrong choice. How could I disgrace the image she (and I) had of missionaries—*real* missionaries? Would she be proud of the way I was treating my uniform? Bless that little girl's heart, whoever she is, for she helped me wear my uniform as a missionary with greater honor and dignity. The most amazing thing, however, was that as I attempted to wear my uniform of Christ with honor and dignity, honor and dignity came to me.

I believe that we can be a great strength to The Church of Jesus Christ of Latter-day Saints if we stand up for our team, keep our uniform of Christ (all of it) on at all times, and learn to wear it worthily. It is not enough, however, to merely wear the uniform. We live in a time where we must do more, be more. We must strive to become letterpersons—persons who make a significant contribution to the success of the Church. John wrote: "He that saith he abideth in [Christ] ought himself also so to walk, even as he walked" (1 John 2:6). May we stand united in our efforts to be strong in the gospel. May we be united in being easily identified as Saints. And may we remain faithful in our thoughts, words, and deeds, in all places, at all times, and in all circumstances as we walk as the Master walked, is my humble hope and prayer.

Matt Richardson teaches at Brigham Young University in the Department of Ancient Scripture. He served a mission to Denmark and later graduated from BYU as Outstanding Senior Man in the communications department. He holds a master's degree and is working toward a doctorate at BYU. Matt serves as a bishop in his Orem, Utah, ward and enjoys sports, traveling, and making Mickey Mouse pancakes on Saturday mornings. He and his wife, Lisa, have three children.

24

"LORD, I BELIEVE;
HELP THOU MINE UNBELIEF"

Kathryn Schlendorf Smith

Mom! I'm really doing this!" My daughter was starting to hyperventilate in the backseat of the car. We were on our way to the Missionary Training Center. She had five suitcases full of an eighteen-month supply of everything a girl could imagine needing. A huge quilt was tied to her pillow, and hangers were tied onto that. All the MTC officials stared at the haul as it came through the doors. She would walk through one door, and with that step her childhood would be over; parental nurturing would be suspended; memories of lazy Saturday mornings and late-night adventures with friends would be packed in boxes with all her possessions, and left in the storage room until she returned.

What did it take to walk through that door into the mission field? What is it taking to stay there? Her companion picked her up that first afternoon at the mission home. They drove deeper and deeper into the inner city. Gang markings blocked out territory. From time to time they witnessed furtive drug sales. More than once when they would return home at night, flashing lights and sirens would announce that someone else on her block had been beaten. She found sadness, poverty, desperation, and despair. The air hung thick in darkness. *What am I doing here?* she wondered.

Her first week she was welcomed by amoebic dysentery. No one invited her to stay in bed and get well. She gobbled pills and worked fourteen hours a day with hungry piranha chomping in her guts. Spiders infested her closets, her clothing, her sheets. The first month, the city sewage backed up and filled the bathtub in her apartment. A month later the pipes broke and flooded the floors. One evening an elder flicked a cockroach out of her long blonde hair, and she wrote that she had become so accustomed to the bugs that she didn't even flinch.

How does she stay? She confesses that she thinks daily about coming home. "There is only one reason I can do this," she wrote. "It is *not* because of social pressure. It certainly is not because it is easy or because I like it." (Of course, she has grown to love the members and investigators whose lives have intertwined with hers. But that alone would not be enough.) "It is only because I love the Lord, and I know this is where I am supposed to be."

"For we walk by faith, not by sight" (2 Corinthians 5:7). By "sight" she would have taken the first plane home. Every day she prays to feel the peace that so many missionaries have spoken of. It doesn't come. She puts on her name tag, grits her teeth, and goes out again. What is missing?

Stepping out of the incredible clouds of eternity, climbing down from Mount Hermon, the mount of Jesus' transfiguration, the Savior and his senior Apostles returned again to Galilee. A blanket of silence lay over the multitude as the scribes mocked his disciples, who had not been successful in casting out an evil spirit. A desperate father stepped forward. With tear-filled eyes, he spoke of his only

son: "Master, I have brought unto thee my son, which hath
a dumb spirit; and wheresoever he taketh him, he teareth
him: and he foameth, and gnasheth with his teeth, and
pineth away: and I spake to thy disciples that they should
cast him out; and they could not" (Mark 9:14–18). Did
Jesus' disciples have faith? They had performed many miracles, even raising the dead. This time they had no power.
What was missing?

Loving, merciful Jesus turned his eyes toward the miserable, pleading father and said, "Bring him unto me."

"And they brought him [the child] unto him: and when
he saw him, straightway the spirit tare him; and he fell on
the ground, and wallowed foaming." This child was
insane. He was a demon, a maniac. The father begged, "If
thou canst do any thing, have compassion on us, and help
us." Certainly, everyone must have been holding their
breath, waiting to see what the Savior would do. Jesus
looked into the eyes of this man and explained what was
missing for his disciples, for my daughter, and perhaps for
you and me.

"If thou canst believe, all things are possible to him that
believeth" (Mark 9:19–23).

When the rubber meets the road, do we believe the Lord
can do it? When the problem seems impossible, do we
believe that Heavenly Father can make it possible? Do we
have faith as a grain of mustard seed? Jesus said that if we
do, we can move mountains (see Matthew 17:20). Or is our
faith comparable in size to atoms or neutrons?

I suggest that all of us echo the desperate yearning
expressed in the words of that anguished father whose
faith was on trial in behalf of his son. "Lord, I believe; help
thou mine unbelief" (Mark 9:24). You and I want our faith
to be the force behind us, but we live in a world where
things we can see and touch and feel seem the most real.
Our job is to learn to exchange "sight" for faith in God.

Peter and several other Apostles were on a ship on the

Sea of Galilee. Peter looked out and saw the Savior walking on the sea, approaching him. He called to Jesus, asking to be permitted to walk on the water with the Lord. Could you or I have done that? Or would we simply have stood there in awe of what we could see the Lord was doing? Would we have had the faith to call out from the ship, "Hey! Can I do that too?"

"Come," was all the Savior said. Peter stepped out onto the waves. What would it have taken to put your weight on that first step? Could you let go of the railing and believe that you could stand on water? By "sight"—through your senses, your experiences, everything you have been taught—you would sink.

Peter let go; he stepped away from the ship and walked toward Jesus. Almost immediately the winds arose. Satan does not cheer when we exercise faith in the Lord. He musters up any trouble he can use to frighten us. Peter looked at the rising waves, lost his courage, and started to sink. "Lord, save me," he cried. Jesus, ever patient, reached out for him. "O thou of little faith, wherefore didst thou doubt?" (Matthew 14:30–31).

My question would come before that. Peter, how did you have the courage to step? We are at different levels of faith, different levels of depending on sight. The Savior invites us to "Come" and walk with him—not to doubt. That is the process and journey of this life.

Sometimes my faith is only the size of a neutron. I want a grain of mustard seed, but I doubt. I doubt myself. I doubt my own worthiness to tap into the power of faith. I make mistakes every day. Why would God honor me? "Lord, I believe" is true. I have had tender personal witnesses that the Spirit is real; that Heavenly Father did exactly what he said he did; that he led the boy Joseph Smith to a quiet, sacred grove of trees and sent Moroni to show him a golden book. I know that through God's power that boy was able to translate the book and to establish a church that is true. I know that. But I cry out almost daily, "Help thou mine unbelief!" as I strive to find the courage to choose what is right, and the will to make it the priority in my life.

As we come to these crossroads, we beg for power, and the Lord mercifully extends it. Our faith increases. Then what? Does our ability to obey and consecrate our lives to him increase? It must in order for the power to come again. Elder Neal A. Maxwell has said, "Another cosmic fact: only by aligning our wills with God's is full happiness to be found. Anything less results in a lesser portion (see Alma 12:10–11). The Lord will work with us even if, at first, we 'can no more than desire' but are willing to 'give place for a portion of [His] words' (Alma 32:27). A small foothold is all He needs! But we must desire and provide it" (*Ensign*, November 1995, p. 23).

God is not distant, the prophets have told us. He is eighteen inches away—the distance from our knees to the floor. Some of us find that quite far. It is like letting go of the ship's rail and stepping out onto the waves simply to kneel and pray, believing that our Father is there. Is that fear of praying perhaps caused by feelings of unworthiness? "Why would the Lord want a miserable wretch like me for a disciple?" we wonder. "Certainly he can find kinder, more righteous followers than I am." And so we *watch* him instead of *joining* him.

A young man was raised by faithful parents. They did the best they knew how to do. Were they perfect? No one is. But they tried. Family prayers were said daily. Family home evenings together were regularly held. This boy was taught the facts of the gospel, but he did not believe. He did not act on his knowledge, and it was dormant in him. In his late teens, in the 1970s, he left home and did not communicate with his family for three years. The police had his photograph and his name, and stats were filed with missing persons departments, but nothing came of the searching. He was simply gone. "What did we do wrong? What more could we have done?" The parents took the blame for their lost son.

The boy drifted from one group of companions to another. Finally he ended up outside a large metropolitan city in a commune of criminally involved individuals. They organized their robberies and their drug deals from a secluded ranch, and the authorities did not know they were there. Anyone who tried to leave the commune was beaten, often to death. This boy knew there was no turning back. It did not take long for him to realize that he had never intended for his life to get to this place. He had just drifted. Now he was in the rapids, and only deadly rocks lay ahead. By "sight" there was no escape.

One night, lying awake in terror, he asked himself again, "What have I done? What can I do?" An image arose in his mind. He saw his mother and father in his living room at home. They were having family home evening. He saw himself on the couch, bored, restless, eager for the lesson to be over. He heard the echo of his mother's words: "God is not distant. He loves you. He will answer your prayers." This young man had not prayed in faith for years. But he heard his mother's voice, and he knew that she believed. He rolled toward the wall, lying on the bottom bunk in a ranch house hidden in some unnamed hills. The night was pitch black. Hot tears bathed his cheeks. He could feel a symbolic wind howling and waves swelling around his heels. For the first time in his life he cried out in his mind, as Peter had, "Lord, save me!"

The words were awkward as he formed them: "Heavenly Father, my mother told me you are not far away. She believes that you are there and that you love me. Can you help me?" Can't we just imagine what that boy must have been thinking? Could all the things he had ever done have flashed across the stage of his mind? By "sight" he might wonder, Why would God love *me*? Why would he be near? Instead, he leaned on the faith of his mother and stepped out onto the water. "Lord, I believe; help thou mine unbelief."

Lying on that bunk in the pitch blackness, the boy did not have to wait long. Almost immediately words came into his mind: "Get out. Get up and leave." By "sight" he asked, "But how?" By "sight" he knew that all the men sleeping in the other bunks would hear him, would stop him, and would beat him for trying to escape. The voice returned and said, "Now." The boy turned over and sat up. He grabbed his boots and tiptoed to the door. All he heard was the snoring of the men. No one stirred. He stepped onto the porch, sure that the dogs would wake up and bark at him. They did not. He crossed the yard to the gate, opened it, pulled on his boots, and ran for all he was worth. He did not stop until he saw the lights of the highway and then only to stick out his thumb. A trucker pulled over and gave him a lift to a nearby gas station, where that boy used the phone. At two o'clock in the morning his parents' phone rang. "Mom and Dad, will you come and get me? I want to come home."

"Lord, I believe; help thou mine unbelief." The Lord is not distant, and he wants to reinforce our faith. We must take that first step. We must believe and ask. All things are possible to him that believeth—to him (or her) who walks not by sight, but by faith.

Is it hard to go to church? Maybe we feel no one likes us there; maybe the lessons are repetitious or boring. Maybe we are tired and it is far; why not just sleep? At a stake conference several years ago, I heard Elder Boyd K. Packer talk of a visit he had made to South America. The members there went to church in a chicken coop. "It wasn't a nice clean chicken coop like we have here in America, either," he explained. The floors were dirt, and not recently cleaned. Why did they go?

Is it hard to pay tithing? Our paycheck barely gets us by;

there is so much we need. One of my missionary daughter's first investigators was an old woman named Antonia. When she was interviewed for baptism by the district leaders, they asked if she would live the law of tithing. This woman works in a sweatshop for a minimum wage. She is in her seventies. Often she is laid off and cannot earn an income. Money is very scarce for her. Her eyes widened in fear as she heard that challenge. "I will," she replied. How did she make that commitment? On the night of her baptism she brought her first payment of tithing. It was her grocery money. The next day there were twenty layoffs in her little factory. Her name was not on the list. She came rejoicing to church on the next Sunday and had another payment of tithing for the bishop.

Is it hard to stay out of inappropriate movies? We hear all those words at school anyway; besides, many people claim that the only good movies are the ones we are supposed to avoid. Is it hard not to date nonmembers? "They have better values than the kids in my ward." "How can I convert anyone if I never go out with them?" You know the arguments. Is it hard to stay on a mission? The conditions are often wretched; it seems nothing we do makes any difference. The Apostle and great missionary Paul wrote a letter from a Roman prison: "But what things were gain to me, those I counted loss for Christ. . . . and I count all things but loss for the excellency of the knowledge of Christ Jesus my Lord: for whom I have suffered the loss of all things, and do count them but dung, that I may win Christ, . . . I count not myself to have apprehended [not to have understood much]: but this one thing I do, forgetting those things which are behind, and reaching forth unto those things which are before, I press toward the mark for the prize of the high calling of God in Christ Jesus" (Philippians 3:7–8, 13).

There is only one reason that can effectively motivate us to follow the prophet: God stands on the other side of those doors and calls to us, "Come." Let go of the ship. Take the first step. Do those things that the prophets have counseled. Walk by faith, not by sight. The Lord is not distant, and he loves us. He will sustain you and me; he will bless us and replace our unbelief with power. Try him.

"The submission of one's will is really the only uniquely personal thing we have to place on God's altar. The many other things we 'give' . . . are actually the things He has already given or loaned to us. However, when you and I finally submit ourselves, by letting our individual wills be swallowed up in God's will, then we are really giving something to Him! It is the only possession which is truly ours to give!" (Neal A. Maxwell, *Ensign,* November 1995, p. 24).

Kathryn Schlendorf Smith joined the Church when she was fifteen years old. She teaches English and French at a middle school in Provo, Utah, and taught early morning seminary for eight years. Kathryn studied for a year in France and traveled the world with a Brigham Young University group in 1966. She has taught at EFY and in other programs since 1983.

25

HOGMET—WHAT TO DO WHEN THEY SAY IT'S NOT TRUE

Brad Wilcox

"Could I ask you a question, even if it doesn't have anything to do with your lesson?" The young woman spoke confidently. I had been teaching the fifteen-year-olds in Sunday School for about a month.

"Sure," I said. Her uncharacteristic seriousness puzzled me. This was the girl who was always talking and laughing with her friends (even during my lessons). What could be so serious that she was now this solemn?

She began. "I have this friend, and the other night we were talking, and he said he doesn't believe in Joseph Smith anymore because Joseph Smith was a gold-digger and a thief and he drank a lot." I smiled. She continued, "My friend has these books to prove it!"

So that was the big, life-and-death matter. This young woman had finally had her first taste of the cold and far-from-nutritious dish called "anti-Mormon literature."

She went on. "Those books—they say the Church isn't true! They say it's a cult and that Joseph Smith was a con man who just made up stories because he wanted power and money and—"

"Hold it," I stopped her. How many reading assignments had I given in the last month that the entire class had ignored? I practically had to turn cartwheels to get these kids to even skim the scriptures, and here this girl was reading entire anti-Mormon books. I faced her. "Not everything you're reading is true."

"But it's in a book," she responded innocently.

"Just because something is printed, sold, and even accepted and popular doesn't make it true," I explained.

"I know that." She was embarrassed. "But how do you know when something you read or hear about the Church is true?" She had raised a good question—especially because we live in a time when so much negative information is widely available.

Moroni once told young Joseph Smith, "They will circulate falsehoods to destroy your reputation, and also will seek to take your life. . . . Persecution [will] rage more and more; for the iniquities of men shall be revealed, and those who are not built upon the Rock will seek to overthrow this church; but it will increase the more [it is] opposed, and spread farther and farther" (*Messenger and Advocate* 2:199).

The angel's words to the Prophet have been and are still being fulfilled. Since 1830, when the Church was organized, over 2,000 anti-Mormon books, novels, movies, pamphlets, tracts, and flyers have been produced in English, with the most dramatic increase in numbers coming since 1960. John W. Welch wrote, "Few other religious groups in the United States have been subjected to such sustained, vitriolic criticism and hostility" (*Encyclopedia of Mormonism*, 5 vols. [New York: Macmillan, 1992], 1:45). Yet through it all the Church continues to grow and progress— just as Moroni foretold.

So how do we know what's true and what isn't? Here is

what my young Sunday School friend and I finally decided: Anything we hear or read about people, practices, ideas, or beliefs needs to pass what we called the HOG-MET test. Each letter stands for a question.

H—Is it hearsay? "Did you know that Steve asked Amy out? I wasn't there myself, but my friend's aunt's cousin's elder's quorum president said . . ." It's interesting to discover that many of the self-appointed critics who claimed (and even signed affidavits) that Joseph Smith and his family were "destitute of moral character," "addicted to vicious habits," and "particularly famous for visionary projects" had never even met the Prophet or his family (see Hugh Nibley, *The Myth Makers* [Salt Lake City: Bookcraft, 1961], p. 12). It seems these people were just passing on something they happened to *hear* someone *say*—hearsay.

O—Is it out of context? It's shocking to hear that the bishop said *damn* in church until we realize he was talking about a fishing trip he took to the reservoir behind the *dam*. Even scriptures and quotes from Church leaders can be misinterpreted if we are not careful to consider the words within their setting and time.

Joseph Smith is sometimes described in anti-Mormon publications as "a young treasure seeker." Out of context, such a statement can be disturbing. However, "treasure seeking" was a common practice in early America. Wasn't treasure the major motivation behind the settlement of Jamestown? Wasn't it gold rushes, in their various forms, that motivated most people who migrated west during the next two centuries? Young Joseph was sometimes employed as a laborer by men who were mining and otherwise seeking treasure, but to call Joseph a "treasure seeker" out of this context does not fairly represent his occupation, motivation, or character.

G—Is it a generalization without evidence? Generalization is a thought process that usually involves insufficient evidence. However, sometimes people are too hasty and they mistakenly accept statements as true when there is little or even no evidence to support them. To believe that *every* member of Joseph Smith's family was ignorant, lazy, and worthless and that *all* the males were blasphemers, liars, and thieves, as some authors have written, is as ridiculous as believing that all North Americans are millionaires or that all Latter-day Saints sing like members of the Tabernacle Choir.

I once listened to a national news interview in which a former Mormon claimed that, like her ex-husband, all Mormon men were authoritarian, dictatorial, domineering, and even abusive. Recognizing that such a hasty generalization was far-fetched, one caller responded, "I live next door to a Mormon couple, and the husband is wonderful. Why blame your former church just because you married a jerk?"

We must be careful. When we hear statements such as "Mormons are prejudiced," "Mormons are perfectionists," "*All* Mormons have large families," or "*All* Mormon women are on medication for depression," we must recognize them for the hasty and unsupported generalizations they are.

M—Is it mudslinging? Competitors, each trying to look better than the other, often attempt to discredit their opponents. The term *mudslinging* dates back to early Roman days when men running for office would wear white togas with purple stripes over their tunics. To show disrespect, their opponents would hire people to throw dirt on the candidates' white robes. Today politicians may not toss literal mud at each other, but they fling a good deal of verbal mud—comments and accusations—to make a mess of each other's images and reputations. Similar dirty tactics are employed in businesses, between high school rivals, and, sadly, even among members of religious denominations.

Were the ministers and scholars who so meanly attacked Joseph Smith innocent of any personal biases? Or were they feeling threatened by the dynamic young Prophet and the truth he bore? Richard Lloyd Anderson wrote, "It is unfortunate that the writers who did the earliest work of gathering information about the Smith family were more concerned with blackening their reputation than with finding the facts" (*Ensign,* August 1987, p. 61). Apostates and enemies of the Church have always stood to lose something if they couldn't find—or put—a little dirt on Latterday Saint white shirts.

E—Is it an exaggeration? I was definitely taken aback when I heard that Brigham Young had more than 400 wives during his lifetime. *Four hundred!* Brigham Young himself would probably be taken aback at that overstatement. We all know that as tales get passed along they get taller. We need to recognize the stretch marks.

One anti-Mormon publication made the outlandish claim that "Mormons own a substantial portion of Hawaii." Was the author referring to individual Latter-day Saints or to the Church itself? Either way, the facts were obviously being distorted. Another publication stated that Utah, with its Mormon population, "ranks among the highest" of the states in teenage pregnancy and venereal diseases. Is everyone living in Utah LDS? Could a high teenage pregnancy rate be partially due to the fact that, with the help offered by priesthood leaders and through Church Social Services, many young couples choose to reveal and continue a pregnancy rather than terminate it through abortion, as some teens do when no such intervention is offered? Or is the information possibly incorrect? According to national statistics from the Atlanta Communicable Disease Center, Utah ranks forty-seventh among the states in venereal disease—hardly "among the highest."

T—Is it true? An unwanted flyer placed under my windshield wiper during a stake conference read, "Before you believe Joseph Smith, read what the Bible says about false prophets."

"Okay," I thought, "but if you're so quick to claim Joseph Smith was a false prophet, where's the real one? Doesn't the Bible also speak of the absolute necessity of latter-day prophets (Amos 3:7) and of a restoration (Acts 3:19)? Didn't Jesus say that false prophets could be recognized by their fruits (Matthew 7:20)? Joseph and all his successors have produced nothing but good, worthy, wholesome, and delicious fruits."

The flyer continued, "Joseph Smith proves himself a liar because he said he saw God face to face."

I thought, "Yes, Joseph *did* claim to see God, but how does that make him a liar? Moses and Stephen made the same claim (see Exodus 33:11; Acts 7:55–56). How come you're not calling *them* liars?" To claim to have seen God would be lying, unless one really had seen him, as Moses, Stephen, and Joseph had. In the exact same way, to claim to be God's son would be blasphemous, unless one really were God's son, as Christ was. Truth is truth, and trying to explain it away or claiming it is impossible cannot change it.

Despite those who refuse to believe, Joseph's first vision cannot be disproved. Joseph wrote, "I had beheld a vision. I have thought since, that I felt much like Paul . . . ; there were but few who believed him; some said he was dishonest, others said he was mad; and he was ridiculed and reviled. But all this did not destroy the reality of his vision. . . .

"So it was with me. I had actually . . . seen a vision; I knew it, and I knew that God knew it, and I could not deny it" (Joseph Smith–History 1:24–25).

Once a nonmember friend who was investigating the Church called me early in the morning. He said his minister had given him some material about the LDS Church, which he had been reading throughout the night. "It has really upset me," he said. "This book says Mormons claim the Bible is incomplete, that there is no salvation outside their Church, that Jesus and Satan are spirit brothers . . ."

As he spoke I reviewed my mental checklist. Was it hearsay, out of context? No. My friend went on. "The book says Mormons believe God created other worlds, and that our Heavenly Father is married—that there is a *mother* in heaven." Was it a hasty generalization? No.

"And Mormons believe the words of their living prophet to be more vital to them than scriptures!" Was it mudslinging or an exaggeration? No. My friend concluded, "Brad, please tell me this isn't true."

I waited silently for a moment and then said, "You may have been reading in an anti-Mormon book, but the things you have just said to me right now might as well have come out of the family home evening manual." Before I even had the chance to explain myself further, my friend quickly ended our phone conversation and his investigation of the Church.

At first I felt terrible. I wondered if perhaps I shouldn't have admitted so quickly that I believed everything my friend had said. However, deep inside, I knew I should have. Elder W. Grant Bangerter wrote, "Now let me make our position clear. Although we should treat others with kindness, tolerance, and respect, we must stand firmly for the things that have been revealed to us. We do not apologize that we do not have the same doctrines and principles that other churches have. We can talk about it in a warm and friendly way, but we do not apologize. We didn't initiate this restoration. God did. If others do not appreciate the Church or its doctrines, we nevertheless know they are true" (*Ensign*, July 1986, p. 71).

I realize that some around the world are horribly offended when we claim divine priesthood authority. I am also aware that it is far from popular or politically correct to affirm that God has not changed his views on Sabbath day observance, profanity, modesty, or chastity. While the world embraces "alternative lifestyles," "changing paradigms," and "multiple realities," we certainly don't sound too sophisticated by claiming to be "the only true and living church" (D&C 1:30). Nevertheless, we stand on testimonies based on experience, study, and personal revelation and remain "true to the faith that our parents have cherished, true to the truth for which martyrs have perished" (*Hymns*, no. 254).

We must not be overly concerned when others choose to spend so much of their time and money fighting against our cause rather than promoting their own. In a way, their efforts serve only as additional evidence of the truthfulness of the Church. It is said that when Benjamin Franklin, as U.S. Ambassador to France, felt misunderstood and persecuted, a friend wrote him a letter saying, "When I see boys in a field throwing rocks at a tree, I know there's fruit on it or they would leave it alone."

President Spencer W. Kimball told the youth, "Do not be puzzled if sometimes there are those in the world who mock how you live and what you believe, saying it is all false, but who, deep inside themselves, are really afraid that what you believe is really true" (*New Era*, April 1980, p. 36).

The Church has always had its critics, and it probably always will. The Savior had his critics too. But for as many as there are who fight against us; for all who would convince us that the Church has no place for "intellectuals" or minorities, and that Mormons devalue women; for all who would suggest that Latter-day Saints are brainwashed and manipulated; for all who may picket Temple Square, denounce Church leaders, and claim that the "spirit" we have felt is of the devil; there are others—millions of others—who stand just as firmly for what is right. Elder Vaughn J. Featherstone said, "The enemies of the Church could line up four abreast from San Francisco to Salt Lake

City and . . . try to convince me that the Church was not true, and when the last one had passed I would still know . . . it is true" (*Hold Up Your Light* [Salt Lake City: Bookcraft, 1986], p. 169). Church leaders, parents, friends, and seminary teachers join living apostles and prophets as witnesses that we are not mistaken or confused. We know who we are, we know the God we worship, and we know what he expects of each of us.

Is it hearsay, out of context, a hasty generalization, mudslinging, or an exaggeration? Is it the truth? HOGMET—it's not a surefire way to wipe out all opposition; rather, it's an easy-to-remember set of questions that will help us keep everything we read and hear about our Church leaders and doctrines in perspective.

My fifteen-year-old friend was ready to leave. She smiled and said, "Next time that guy ever says he has another book for me to read, I'll have a few questions for him first."

"Good luck," I offered.

"Oh, I won't need luck." She started off down the hall. "Now I have HOGMET!"

Brad Wilcox, a popular youth speaker and author, teaches at Brigham Young University. He served a mission to Chile and has traveled all over the world. He holds a Ph.D. degree from the University of Wyoming and serves as an executive board member for the Boy Scouts of America. Brad and his wife, Debi, have four children.